PRACTICAL SPELLING

THE BAD SPELLER'S GUIDE
TO GETTING IT RIGHT EVERY TIME

Anna Castley

LEARNINGEXPRESS

NEW YORK

Library of Congress Cataloging-in-Publication Data

Castley, Anna.
    Practical spelling/Anna Castley.
      p.   cm. — (The basics made easy)
    ISBN 1-57685-083-8
    1. English language—Orthography and spelling—Problems, exercises, etc.
  I. Title. II. Series
PE1145.2.C37   1998
428.1—dc21   97–39166
                                CIP

Printed in the United States of America
9 8 7 6 5 4 3 2 1
First Edition

For Further Information
For information on LearningExpress, other LearningExpress products, or bulk sales,
please call or write to us at:
    LearningExpress®
    900 Broadway
    Suite 604
    New York, NY 10003
    212-995-2566

LearningExpress is an affiliated company of Random House, Inc.

Distributed to the retail trade by Random House, Inc., as agent for LearningExpress, LLC
Visit LearningExpress on the World Wide Web at www.learnx.com

ISBN 1-57685-083-8

CONTENTS

INTRODUCTION

How you greet someone depends on where you come from.

Americans use the word *hello*.

Italians use the words *buon giorno*.

Egyptians use the words *al salaam*.

The letters in the words of greeting are symbols in each native language, arranged in specific ways for successful communication. That's what spelling is. Spelling is the vehicle that carries the thoughts in your mind to paper. So, if you want to communicate your thoughts on paper for others to read, you need to spell correctly. This is true in any language.

Improving your spelling for self-improvement and professional growth is an important decision. You've made that decision; now it's time to follow through and learn the techniques you need to become a good speller.

HOW TO USE THIS BOOK

The following are some tips that will help you use this book successfully to improve your spelling.

- Record your answers to the questions and the exercises in this book, or, particularly if this book does not belong to you, purchase a notebook just for your spelling improvement. The answers should be recorded lesson by lesson. You will be able to see your spelling skills develop as each lesson is introduced.

- Obtain a dictionary. You will encounter unfamiliar words—don't let them slide by you. Reach for your dictionary, look those words up, and understand their meaning.

- Purchase a red pencil or a highlighter marker. You'll need it to circle letters and to write slash marks (/).

- Ask a friend to be your study buddy. This person will dictate words or sentences to you for spelling practice. If you have a tape recorder, be creative and make it your study buddy.

- Find a place where you can read **aloud**. Since you will be listening to yourself to identify and compare sounds, you must be comfortable reading aloud.

- Set a specific time for each lesson. Each lesson is designed to be completed in 20 minutes, though you may take more or less time with some lessons. If you spend 20 minutes a day with this book, you can improve your spelling skills in just 20 days. You may want to set aside the same block of time each day. This commitment to yourself will keep you working consistently towards your goal.

WHAT IS IN EACH LESSON?

Each lesson introduces 10 or more spelling words, selected to help you learn each lesson's particular spelling skill or strategy.

Each Exercise 1 throughout this book instructs you to look closely at the differences in words and locate their common letters. When you see this picture of an eye-hand connection, it symbolizes looking carefully across a line of words. This is called **eyeballing the spelling words**. Sometimes you will be instructed to circle the one word in a line that doesn't match the others. Other times you'll be asked to circle the common letters in the remaining words. This eye-hand movement allows you to see the similarities and differences in words.

Each Exercise 2 throughout this book asks you to take a **sound inventory.** When you see this picture of an ear in this book, it symbolizes listening. To do this exercise successfully, you must read the group of words **aloud** because you are listening for a common sound. Your study buddy could read the words to you as you listen for the common sound. Be comfortable about reading **aloud**—these exercises are very helpful, but will get you little or nothing if you whisper them or simply sound them out in your head. Stating them clearly in a normal speaking voice will yield the best results.

A picture of a mirror follows some exercises in this book. This picture symbolizes **reflection.** When you see it, you should think about the exercises it appears beside. The reflection symbol also requires you to write about your thoughts. Thinking over the exercises helps you understand the new spelling skill and summarize what you have learned.

There are two exercises in each lesson that help you practice the new spelling words. This picture of a hand holding a pencil means to grab that pencil and start writing! It's important to write the words as often as you can and practice writing them in context. The word *context* means to use the spelling word correctly in a sentence. Refer to the **Letter/Sound Relationship Key** (later in this Introduction) to help you remember the letters that represent the sound. If you're unsure what a word means, be sure to use your dictionary to look it up.

The lessons in this book are designed to teach you spelling skills. If you truly understand the skills you can apply them to other words in your daily life. You'll meet new words every day. Unfortunately, there's one problem with spelling skills in the English language—they're not always consistent. As soon as you learn a spelling skill there are variations and exceptions to it. So just be aware that the skills don't work perfectly all the time. When you see the word VARIATIONS in the lesson, it means what you have just learned **is not true all the time.**

Beginning with Lesson 2, this symbol means that the nearby letter/sound relationship appears in more challenging words. Practice writing the words in your notebook and make a commitment to use them in your oral and written language.

Each lesson ends with a review and practice exercise called What Have You Learned? The repetition in each review reinforces the spelling skill you have learned, and the answer key at the end of the lesson allows you to check yourself and evaluate how you're doing.

WHAT YOU MUST KNOW BEFORE LESSON 1

The English language uses an alphabet with 26 letters. The arrangement of these letters spells words that convey meaning. This book refers to the letters *a, e, i, o, u,* and sometimes *y* as **vowels.** These vowels are also called long and short vowels for the sounds they represent. The remaining letters are called **consonants.**

Each letter (or letters) represents a sound. String two or more letters together and you will write a simple word like *so,* or a syllable like *de.* A syllable can be a real word or part of a word. **A word can only be a word and a syllable can only be a syllable if it has a vowel.** So answer this question. Can a vowel be a syllable? Of course it can, because it is a vowel. A vowel can stand alone but a consonant cannot. The word *open* has two syllables and can be separated into two syllables like this: *o-pen.* The vowel can stand alone.

Vowels can make either a long or a short sound. Here are two general rules that apply most of the time.

1. If a vowel ends a syllable like the letter *u* in the word *mu-sic,* it usually has a long /u/ sound. This is called an open syllable.
2. If a vowel sits between two consonants like the vowel letter *i* in *mu-sic* or the *i* in *lin-en* it usually has a short /i/ vowel sound. This is called a closed syllable.

To help you hear the letter/sound relationship of the consonants and vowels within syllables or words, read the **Letter/Sound Relationship Key** that begins on page 7 out loud. The clue words on the list will help you hear the sounds. When a letter appears in italics like this, *s,* it means the **letter**. When a letter appears between slash marks like this, /s/, it means the **sound.**

USING THE LETTER/SOUND RELATIONSHIP KEY

On the last pages of this Introduction, you will see a letter/sound relationship key that you will be asked to refer to many times as you work through this book. The key is set up so that you can cut it out for easy reference as you work through this book. Of course, **if this book does not belong to you, don't cut out the pages!**

Read the consonant key and the vowel keys aloud. Listen for the sounds each letter or letters make. Do this many times. You're likely to be more comfortable doing this if you're in a private, quiet place. While you're reading aloud, you need to listen to yourself and then write what you hear.

The letters you select when you write a word determine whether the word is spelled correctly. To put it another way, spelling is putting the correct letters together so others who read your writing will understand your message. Communication occurs when all writers and readers agree on the same letter/sound relationship, and using the letter/sound relationship key on the following pages will help you do this.

You are asked to use this letter/sound strategy many times in the exercises in this book. This strategy will enhance your ability to use sounds as a spelling skill. As an example, the letter/sound relationship for the word *rat* is /r/a/t/. It has three sounds and three letters to represent the sound. The letter/sound relationship for the word *light* is /l/i/t/. You can hear only three sounds in the word *light,* but there are five letters. The letters *g* and *h* are silent. Read the following list carefully for more examples of the letter/sound relationship strategy.

grandstand	/g/r/a/n/d/s/t/a/n/d/	You hear all the letters in this word.
elbow	/e/l/b/o/	You don't hear the letter *w*.
brave	/b/r/a/v/	You don't hear the letter *e*.

This type of exercise is meant to sharpen your listening ability.

GETTING STARTED

So you've decided to improve your spelling because you found out spelling will greatly influence what you say and how you say it. How much do you know about spelling skills? How can you build on what you already know? Asking yourself these two questions is how a learner learns. Learning is a process of construction, like building a house. Once you start, there's no end to the things you can build.

Get your tools and your notebook and let's start the construction process!

THE LETTER/SOUND RELATIONSHIP KEY

CONSONANTS

Each consonant letter represents a sound. The example, or clue word, will help you hear and remember the sound of the letter. Just say the clue word for the letter *b* is *book* because the /b/ sound is the first sound in the word *book*. This is called the letter/sound relationship. Consonants in the letter/sound relationship can appear anywhere in a word. For easy sound recognition, the word clue in the list below represents the **first** sound in the word, but the consonant can be a part of a syllable anywhere in the word.

The Letter	Represents the Sound	Example
b	/b/	The first sound in *book*
c	/k/	The first sound in *cake*
c	/s/	The first sound in *city*
d	/d/	The first sound in *dice*
f	/f/	The first sound in *fork*
g	/g/	The first sound in *goat*
g	/j/	The first sound in *giraffe*
h	/h/	The first sound in *hamburger*
j	/j/	The first sound in *jet*
k	/k/	The first sound in *key*
l	/l/	The first sound in *lemon*
m	/m/	The first sound in *mailbox*
n	/n/	The first sound in *needle*
p	/p/	The first sound in *paper*
q	/k/w/	The first sound in *quilt*
r	/r/	The first sound in *radio*
s	/s/	The first sound in *sun*
t	/t/	The first sound in *telephone*
v	/v/	The first sound in *van*
w	/w/	The first sound in *watch*
x	/k/s/	The first sound in *x-ray*
y	/y/	The first sound in *yacht*
z	/z/	The first sound in *zebra*

When two consonants are side by side, each making their own sound, they form a **consonant blend**. There are *l blends*, *r blends*, and *s blends*. Say the word **cloud** aloud. You can hear the first two sounds. They are represented by the letters *c* and *l*. The following is a list of other sounds that represent consonant blends.

L Blends	/b/l/, /c/l/, /f/l/, /g/l/, /p/l/, /s/l/
R Blends	/b/r/, /c/r/, /d/r/, /f/r, /g/r/, /p/r/, /s/t/r/, /s/p/r/, /t/r/
S Blends	/s/c/, /s/k/, /s/l/, /s/m/, /s/n/, /s/p/, /s/q/u/, /s/t/, /s/w/

Note that /s/l/ can be labeled either an *s* blend or an *l* blend.

VOWELS

Each vowel letter (*a, e, i, o, u,* and sometimes *y*) has a long and short sound, depending on whether the vowel is in an open or closed syllable. The combination of the letters provides a hint about whether the vowel sound is long or short. A combination of vowel letters or a vowel with a consonant can also represent a sound. For easy sound recognition, the clue word in the following vowel key will help you hear the sound. Read this list **aloud** and listen for the sounds.

Short Vowel *a*

The Letter	Represents the Sound	Example
a	/a/	The first sound in *at*
a	/a/	The first, closed syllable in *van-ish*

Long Vowel *a*

The Letters	Represent the Sound	Example
a_e	/a/	The word *cane*
ai	/a/	The word *rain*
ay	/a/	The word *say*
ey	/a/	The word *they*
ei	/a/	The word *eight*
a	/a/	The first syllable in *a-pron*
a	/a/	The first syllable in *ra-zor*

Short Vowel *e*

The Letter	Represents the Sound	Example
e	/e/	The first sound in *egg*
e	/e/	The first, closed syllable in *relish*

Long Vowel *e*

The Letters	Represent the Sound	Example
e_e	/e/	The word *Pete*
ee	/e/	The word *feel*
ea	/e/	The word *seat*
y	/e/	The word *baby*
ie	/e/	The word *chief*

Short Vowel *i*

The Letter	Represents the Sound	Example
i	/i/	The first sound in the word *ill*
i	/i/	The first, closed syllable in *wizard*

Long Vowel *i*

The Letters	Represent the Sound	Example
i_e	/i/	The word *mine*
ie	/i/	The word *pie*
igh	/i/	The word *light*
y	/i/	The word *by*

Short Vowel *o*

The Letter	Represents the Sound	Example
o	/o/	The first sound in *ox*
o	/o/	The first, closed syllable in *model*

Long Vowel *o*

The Letters	Represent the Sound	Example
o_e	/o/	The word *cone*
oa	/o/	The word *coat*
oe	/o/	The word *toe*
ow	/o/	The word *snow*

ol	/o/	The word *cold*
oll	/o/	The word *roll*
ough	/o/	The word *dough*

Short Vowel *u*

The Letter	Represents the Sound	Example
u	/u/	The first sound in *up*
u	/u/	The first, closed syllable in *pun-ish*

Long Vowel *u*

The Letters	Represent the Sound	Example
u_e	/u/	The word *cube*
ue	/u/	The word *blue*
ew	/u/	The word *flew*
ui	/u/	The word *fruit*
oo	/u/	The word *food*

LESSON | 1

Your first twenty minutes will be spent very wisely. You will compare words, listen for sounds, and begin to learn how to use what you already know.

GETTING STARTED

EXERCISE 1: EYEBALLING SPELLING LIST 1

Directions: Sweep your eyes across the line from left to right and back again. Do it quickly. Circle the word in each line that looks different from the others on that line.

Are you ready? Get set . . . Go!

1. lottery   lottery   lottery   pottery
2. number   lumber   lumber   lumber
3. computes   computer   computer   computer
4. remote   remote   remote   remove
5. deplete   deplete   delete   dcplete
6. matter   matter   matter   manner
7. members   mobsters   members   members

8. compile	compile	compile	combine
9. rebate	retrace	rebate	rebate
10. slippers	sippers	slippers	slippers

Check your answers with the answer key at the end of this lesson.
My score for Exercise 1 is _____ out of 10.

REFLECTION

What did you notice about yourself as your eyes moved across the line?

_____

What can you say about how the words compare to each other?

_____

If you said that there were times that all the words on the line looked the same, that's okay. This exercise is designed to make you look at words very closely, because just one letter can change the spelling and the meaning of a word. If you're going to improve your spelling ability, you must see the fine differences in words. Did you see that the words *lottery* and *pottery* are the same except for the first consonant letter? The same is true for *lumber* and *number*. Did you see that the word *deplete* has the consonant blend /p/l/ and *delete* does not?

Move on to Exercise 2, Sound Inventory, to hear the sounds in words.

EXERCISE 2: SOUND INVENTORY

Directions: Listen to yourself as you read each group of words **aloud**. **You must read the words out loud.** There is something that the words in each group have in common. Can you hear it? If not, say the words slowly or have your study buddy read them to you.

GROUP 1	GROUP 2	GROUP 3
main	feet	die
race	Pete	pile
say	be	light
_____	_____	_____

GROUP 4	GROUP 5
toast	sue
bone	suit
doe	rule
_____	_____

Take your red pencil or highlighter and circle the second letter in each word; then write the letter on the line below each group.

In Group 1, the common letter is *a*.

In Group 2, the common letter is *e*.

In Group 3, the common letter is *i*.

In Group 4, the common letter is *o*.

In Group 5, the common letter is *u*.

The *a, e, i, o,* and *u* that you circled are called **long vowels**. Read each word again and listen for the long vowel sounds.

Now look at more groups representing different sounds.

GROUP 6	**GROUP 7**	**GROUP 8**
pit	mat	pest
lip	band	deck
bill	ham	bet
___	___	___

GROUP 9	**GROUP 10**
lot	puff
jog	jug
pond	numb
___	___

Take your red pencil or highlighter and circle the second letter in each word; then write the letter on the line below each group.

In Group 1, the common letter is *i*.

In Group 2, the common letter is *a*.

In Group 3, the common letter is *e*.

In Group 4, the common letter is *o*.

In Group 5, the common letter is *u*.

The *a, e, i, o,* and *u* that you circled are called **short vowels**. Read each word again and listen for the short vowel sounds.

Move on to Exercise 3 to practice writing the vowels and consonants you hear.

EXERCISE 3: PRACTICE WRITING LETTERS AND SOUNDS

Directions: Listen to yourself as you read each group of words **aloud**.

You must read the words aloud. Write the letters that represent the sound you hear, separating them with a slash mark (/). In some cases, there will be more letters than sounds, so be careful. Use the letter/sound relationship key in the Introduction to help you remember the letters and sounds. A few have been done for you.

1. base /b/a/s/	**13.** sue ____	**22.** pest ____
2. trade ____	**14.** suit ____	**23.** desk ____
3. sway ____	**15.** cute ____	**24.** bet ____
4. sweet /s/w/e/t/	**16.** pit ____	**25.** lot ____
5. Pete ____	**17.** slip ____	**26.** jog ____
6. be ____	**18.** bill ____	**27.** pond ____
7. die /d/i/	**19.** mat ____	**28.** stuff ____
8. pie ____	**20.** grand ____	**29.** jug ____
9. high ____	**21.** scam ____	**30.** nut ____
10. toast ____		
11. bone ____		
12. doe ____		

Check your answers with the answer key at the end of this lesson.
My score for Exercise 3 is _____ out of 30.

REFLECTION

What did you find out about letters and sounds?

_____

What did you find out about vowels?

_____

By now you must have realized that spelling has a great deal to do with letters and sounds. Letters and sounds have a very special relationship. There are 26 letters in the English alphabet representing over forty sounds. The letters *a,e,i,o,u* and sometimes *y* are called **vowels**. In Exercise 2, Sound Inventory, you practiced listening for vowel sounds. In groups 1–5 you were asked to listen for the long vowel sounds, and in groups 6–10 you were asked to listen for the short vowel sounds. In the succeeding lessons, you'll have many opportunities to learn how to use the vowel sounds to sharpen your spelling strategies.

The remaining letters in the alphabet are called **consonants**. Consonants and vowels are put together to make syllables or words. **Using the correct letters to represent sounds is spelling.**

In the lessons to follow, you will be introduced to these letters and sounds in a systematic pattern. Spelling will be made easy. The 20 minutes you invest daily will provide you with the skills you need to master the art of spelling.

Move to Exercises 4 and 5 to practice what you've learned about letters and sounds. You will review words from Spelling List 1 from the beginning of this lesson.

EXERCISE 4: PRACTICE WRITING SPELLING LIST 1

Directions: Go back to Exercise 1. Look at the three words that are the same on each line. Write each of these words only once on the lines below. This would be a good time to have your study buddy dictate the words to you.

1. _____   6. _____
2. _____   7. _____
3. _____   8. _____
4. _____   9. _____
5. _____   10. _____

Consult your dictionary if the meaning of a word is unfamiliar to you.

Check your answers with the answer key at the end of this lesson.

My score for Exercise 4 is _____ out of 10.

EXERCISE 5: PRACTICE WRITING SPELLING LIST 1 IN CONTEXT

Directions: Use the words in Exercise 4 to complete each of the following phrases. For added practice, rewrite the entire phrase in your own sentence on the provided line. The first one has been done for you.

1. a winning _lottery_ ticket

   The winning lottery ticket will be announced at 8:00.

2. a five-dollar _____

   _____

3. turn on the _____

   _____

4. the _____ control

   _____

5. a team of 5 _____

_____

6. _____ the data

_____

7. comfortable leather _____

_____

8. _____ natural resources

_____

9. discuss this urgent _____

_____

10. _____ for the wooden deck

_____

Check your answers with the answer key at the end of this lesson. Only the words that go in the blanks are given since everyone will create different sentences.

My score for Exercise 5 is _____ out of 10.

Move on to Exercise 6 to review what you have learned.

EXERCISE 6: WHAT HAVE YOU LEARNED?

1. How many letters are in the English alphabet? _____

2. About how many sounds do those letters represent?

_____

3. What letters represent the short vowel sounds?

_____

4. What letters represent the long vowel sounds? _____

5. Write the letters that represent the sounds in the word *grow.*

_____

6. What is the difference between the words *paddle* and *puddle*?

_____

7. What is the difference between *matter* and *manner*?

_____

How has each word changed?

8. matter/batter

_____

9. rebate/debate

_____

10. remote/remove

_____

Check your answers with the answer key at the end of this lesson.
My score for Exercise 6 is _____ out of 10.

ANSWER KEY FOR LESSON 1

Exercise 1

1. pottery
2. number
3. computes
4. remove
5. delete
6. manner
7. mobsters
8. combine
9. retrace
10. sippers

16. /p/i/t/
17. /s/l/i/p/
18. /b/i/l/
19. /m/a/t/
20. /g/r/a/n/d/
21. /s/c/a/m/
22. /p/e/s/t/
23. /d/e/s/k/
24. /b/e/t/
25. /l/o/t/
26. /j/o/g/
27. /p/o/n/d/
28. /s/t/u/f/
29. /j/u/g/
30. /n/u/t/

Exercise 3

1. /b/a/s/
2. /t/r/a/d/
3. /s/w/a/
4. /s/w/e/t/
5. /p/e/t/
6. /b/e/
7. /d/i/
8. /p/i/
9. /h/i/
10. /t/o/s/t/
11. /b/o/n/
12. /d/o/
13. /s/u/
14. /s/u/t/
15. /c/u/t/

Exercise 4

1. lottery
2. lumber
3. computer
4. remote
5. deplete
6. matter
7. members
8. compile
9. rebate
10. slippers

Exercise 5

1. lottery
2. rebate
3. computer
4. remote
5. members
6. compile
7. slippers
8. deplete
9. matter
10. lumber

Exercise 6

1. 26 letters
2. 40+ sounds
3. *a,e,i,o,u,* and sometimes *y*
4. *a,e,i,o,u,* and sometimes *y*
5. /g/r/o/
6. The vowels (or the second letters) are different.
7. The consonants (letters in the middle) are different.
8. The first consonant changed.
9. The first consonant changed.
10. The last consonant (next to the last letter) changed.

LESSON | 2

There are many short, easy words you already know how to spell. Some longer words are composed of two or more short words; these are called **compound words**. This lesson helps you build your pool of spelling words by showing you some compound words with short vowel sounds.

COMPOUNDING WITH SHORT VOWELS

EXERCISE 1: EYEBALLING SPELLING LIST 2

Directions: Sweep your eyes across the line from left to right and back again. Do it quickly. Circle the word in each line that looks different from the others on that line.

Are you ready? Get set . . . Go!

1. bandstand	bandstand	bandstand	handstand
2. sunsuit	sunset	sunset	sunset
3. handset	headset	handset	handset
4. desktop	diskette	desktop	desktop
5. bedpan	bedpan	bedbug	bedpan
6. inlet	inlet	inlet	islet
7. laptop	laptop	laptops	laptop

8. hotel	hotdog	hotdog	hotdog
9. upset	setup	upset	upset
10. uplift	uplift	updraft	uplift

Check your answers with the answer key at the end of this lesson.
My score for Exercise 1 is _____ out of 10.

REFLECTION

Look carefully at the remaining three words on each line in Exercise 1.
There's something similar about the way these words are put together.
Can you see a pattern? _____ What is the pattern? _____
_____

If you said that all the words are a combination of two words put
together, you're correct. The words in this special group are called
compound words. Compound words are two words written together to
make one word. The following words are common compound words
you use all the time, separated into two words. Thousands of words in
the English language are compound words. They're easy to spell, espe-
cially if you use what you already know.

eyelash	eye	lash
bedroom	bed	room
bathroom	bath	room

Move on to Exercise 2, Sound Inventory, to hear the sounds of this lesson.

EXERCISE 2: SOUND INVENTORY

Directions: Listen for a vowel sound in each group of words. Read each
group of words **aloud** or have your study buddy read them to you. Listen
for the same sound in each word. Find and circle the letter that represents
the vowel sound in each word, then write the letter on the line below each
group of words that represents the sound. What can you say about the
letter/sound relationship in each group?

GROUP 1	**GROUP 2**	**GROUP 3**
band	bell	milk
pan	desk	pin
lap	men	print
_____	_____	_____

GROUP 4	**GROUP 5**
top	stunt
stop	but
clog	nut
_____	_____

In Group 1, the common letter is *a*. Can you hear the sound of the letter *a?* If you need help, break the words up into sounds using slash marks. The word *band* should look like /b/a/n/d/. Now can you hear the sound? It has the same sound as the first sound you hear in the clue word **apple.**

In Group 2, the common letter is *e*. Can you hear the sound of the letter *e?* If you need help, break the words up into sounds using slash marks. The word *desk* should look like /d/e/s/k/. Now can you hear the sound? It has the same sound as the first sound you hear in the clue word *egg.*

In Group 3, the common letter is *i*. Can you hear the sound of the letter *i?* If you need help, break the words up into sounds using slash marks. The word *milk* should look like /m/i/l/k/. Now can you hear the sound? It has the same sound as the first sound you hear in the clue word *ill.*

In Group 4, the common letter is *o*. Can you hear the sound of the letter *o?* If you need help, break the words up into sounds using slash marks. The word *clog* should look like /c/l/o/g/. Now can you hear the sound? It has the same sound as the first sound you hear in the clue word *ox.*

In Group 5, the common letter is *u*. Can you hear the sound of the letter *u?* If you need help, break the words up into sounds using slash marks. The word *nut* should look like /n/u/t/. Now can you hear the sound? It has the same sound as the first sound you hear in the clue word *up.*

These sounds are referred to as **short vowel sounds**. The words *apple, egg, ill, ox,* and *up* are clue words to help you remember the sound. You can choose your own clue words as well.

 ## REFLECTION

How will the clue words help you with short vowel sounds?

_____

What is a compound word?

_____

How are compound words formed?

_____

Do you think compound words can have short vowel sounds?

_____

Clue words can help you remember short vowel sounds. You might want to choose your own clue words instead of the preceding examples—use whatever word will help you remember the sound. A compound word is two smaller words written together as one larger word. Yes, the short vowel sounds you heard in Exercise 2 can be a part of compound words. Move on to Exercise 3 to practice using short vowels within compound words.

EXERCISE 3: USING THE CORRECT SHORT VOWEL

Directions: The following is another list of commonly used compound words. A short vowel, /a/, /e/, /i/, /o/, or /u/, is missing from each word. Write the correct short vowel to complete each word.

1. airer _ ft
2. g _ mstone
3. treadm _ ll
4. n _ twork
5. r _ dwood
6. b _ ttlefield
7. h _ ndshake
8. l _ pstick
9. p _ thway
10. salesm _ n

11. b _ ckground
12. h _ ndwriting
13. livest _ ck
14. pean _ t
15. sawd _ st
16. broadc _ st
17. headh _ nter
18. _ pscale
19. w _ bsite
20. m _ nhole

Check your answers with the answer key at the end of this lesson.
My score for Exercise 3 is _____ out of 20.

EXERCISE 4: PRACTICE WRITING SPELLING LIST 2

Directions: Go back to Exercise 1. Look at the three words that are the same on each line. Write each of the words that are the same only once on the lines. This would be a good time to have your study buddy dictate the words to you.

1. _____	6. _____
2. _____	7. _____
3. _____	8. _____
4. _____	9. _____
5. _____	10. _____

Consult your dictionary if the meaning of a word is unfamiliar to you. Check your answers with the answer key at the end of this lesson.

My score for Exercise 4 is _____ out of 10.

EXERCISE 5: PRACTICE SPELLING LIST 2 IN CONTEXT

Directions: Use any word in Exercise 4 to complete each of the following phrases. For added practice, rewrite the entire phrase in your own sentence on the provided line. The first one has been done for you.

1. a _bedpan_ for the patient
   The nurse provided a bedpan for the patient.

2. hold the _____ and dial
   _____

3. a _____ computer
   _____

4. music from the _____
   _____

5. _____ about the bad news
   _____

6. _____ publishing
   _____

7. _____ your mood with music
   _____

8. a boat in the _____
   _____

9. a glowing _____ at 7:30
   _____

10. eat the _____
   _____

Check your answers with the answer key at the end of this lesson. Only the words that go in the blanks are given, since everyone will create different sentences.

My score for Exercise 5 is _____ out of 10.

VARIATIONS

In some words, the short vowel /e/ (the sound you hear in the clue word *egg*) can be spelled with the letters *ea*, as in the clue word *head*. The following is a list of other words that use *ea*.

bread	steady	ready	dead
wealth	health	feather	weather
deaf	dread	spread	sweat
pleasant	meant	head	

In the words below, the short vowel /i/ (the sound you hear in the clue word *itch*) can be spelled with the letter *y*.

gypsy	gyp	sympathy
gymnasium	mystery	

In some words, the letter *i* can also represent the sound of the consonant /y/ (the sound you hear in the clue word *yes*).

valiant	William	familiar
union	peculiar	brilliant

Practice writing these variations in your notebook or have your study buddy dictate them to you.

Do you want more challenging compound words with short vowel sounds? Try these! Call on your study buddy to dictate them to you and write them in your notebook.

touchpad	sweatshop	sweatband
featherbed	breadbasket	deadbeat
bedspread	shoplifter	spreadsheet

EXERCISE 6: WHAT HAVE YOU LEARNED?

Directions: Go back to Exercise 1. Look at the words that are the same on each line. Write the compound words that are the same only once following blank lines, and then put a slash mark (/) between the two words. On the lines next to each word, write the letters that represent the sounds you hear. The first one is done for you. Check your answers with the answer key at the end of this lesson.

1. band/stand   /b/a/n/d/s/t/a/n/d/ _____
2. _____
3. _____
4. _____
5. _____
6. _____
7. _____
8. _____
9. _____
10. _____

Now go back to each word and locate the vowel. Circle the vowel in each part of the compound word. Remember: the letters that represent the vowels are *a, e, i, o, u,* and sometimes *y.*

11. What vowel sound do you hear in the word *stamp*?_____
What clue word will help you remember the sound?

_____

12. What vowel sound do you hear in the word *pump*? _____
What clue word will help you remember the sound?

_____

13. What vowel sound do you hear in the word *kiss*? _____
What clue word will help you remember the sound?

_____

14. What vowel sound do you hear in the word *elf*? _____
What clue word will help you remember the sound?

_____

15. What vowel sound do you hear in the word *drop*? _____
What clue word will help you remember the sound?

_____

Directions: Separate the two words in the compound words listed below. Write the two words on the line.

16. pathway   _____   _____
17. upscale   _____   _____
18. redwood   _____   _____
19. handshake   _____   _____
20. gemstone   _____   _____

Check your answers with the answer key at the end of this lesson.

My score for Exercise 6 is _____ **out of 20.**

ANSWER KEY FOR LESSON 2
Exercise 1

1. handstand
2. sunsuit
3. headset
4. diskette
5. bedbug
6. islet
7. laptops
8. hotel
9. setup
10. updraft

12. handwriting
13. livestock
14. peanut
15. sawdust
16. broadcast
17. headhunter
18. upscale
19. website
20. manhole

Exercise 3

1. aircraft
2. gemstone
3. treadmill
4. network
5. redwood
6. battlefield
7. handshake
8. lipstick
9. pathway
10. salesman, salesmen
11. background

Exercise 4

1. bandstand
2. sunset
3. handset
4. desktop
5. bedpan
6. inlet
7. laptop
8. hotdog
9. upset
10. uplift

Exercise 5

1. bedpan
2. handset
3. laptop
4. bandstand
5. upset
6. desktop
7. uplift
8. inlet
9. sunset
10. hotdog

Exercise 6

1. band/stand /b/a/n/d/s/t/a/n/d/
2. sun/set /s/u/n/s/e/t/
3. hand/set /h/a/n/d/s/e/t/
4. desk/top /d/e/s/k/t/o/p/
5. bed/pan /b/e/d/p/a/n/
6. in/let /i/n/l/e/t/
7. lap/top /l/a/p/t/o/p/
8. hot/dog /h/o/t/d/o/g/
9. up/set /u/p/s/e/t/
10. up/lift /u/p/l/i/f/t/
11. short /a/ as in the clue word *apple*
12. short /u/ as in the clue word *up*
13. short /i/ as in the clue word *ill*
14. short /e/ as in the clue word *egg*
15. short /o/ as in the clue word *ox*
16. path   way
17. up   scale
18. red   wood
19. hand   shake
20. gem   stone

LESSON | 3

This lesson continues to expand your pool of spelling words by combining words that you already know how to spell with long vowel sound strategies.

COMPOUNDING WITH LONG VOWELS

 EXERCISE 1: EYEBALLING SPELLING LIST 3

Directions: Sweep your eyes across the line from left to right and back again. Do it quickly. Circle the word in each line that looks different from the others on that line.

Are you ready? Get set . . . Go!

1. homestyle   homestyle   homework   homestyle
2. bluejay   bluejay   bluebell   bluejay
3. dewdrop   drewdrop   dewdrop   dewdrop
4. sunlight   sunlight   sunlight   midnight
5. grapenuts   grapefruit   grapefruit   grapefruit
6. rowboats   rowboat   rowboat   rowboat
7. payday   playboy   payday   payday

8.	raindrops	rainfalls	raindrops	raindrops
9.	keepsake	knapsack	keepsake	keepsake
10.	streamline	steamline	streamline	streamline

Check your answers with the answer key at the end of this lesson.

My score for Exercise 1 is _____ out of 10.

REFLECTION

Look at the three words in each line that are the same in Exercise 1. Do you recognize the two words that make up the compound words? _____ What parts of those compound words are a challenge for you? Write any of the shorter words that give you difficulty on the following lines.

_____

_____

Move on to Exercise 2, Sound Inventory, to hear the sounds of this lesson.

EXERCISE 2: SOUND INVENTORY

Directions: Read each group of words **aloud** or have your study buddy read them to you. Listen for a common vowel sound in each group. Write the letters that represent that sound on the lines provided.

GROUP 1	GROUP 2	GROUP 3
grape /g/r/a/p/	easy /e/z/e/	tie /t/i/
pay	stream	dye
rain	keep	light
day	Pete	line
sake	steamy	by
_____	_____	_____

GROUP 4	GROUP 5
home /h/o/m/	cue /c/u/
toe	blue
row	food
boat	dew
code	fruit
_____	_____

In Group 1, the common letter is *a*. Can you hear the sound of the letter *a?* Break the words into sounds using slash marks and write them next to the words. Which letters make no sound at all? _____ The sound you heard in Group 1 is the long vowel /a/, and it makes the sound of its own name, "a." For spelling, the long vowel /a/ can be represented by three combinations of letters—*a_e, ay,* and *ai.* You can use the clue word *day* to help you remember the sound.

Each of the following words is missing a long vowel /a/ combination. Practice the long vowel /a/ combinations of *a_e, ai,* and *ay* by writing them in the blank spaces. Rewrite the whole word on the line provided.

1. dressm _ k _ r _____   **3.** p _ _ d _ _ _____
2. st _ g _ coach _____   **4.** r _ _ drop _____

In Group 2, the common letter is *e*. Can you hear the sound of the letter *e?* Break the words into sounds using slash marks and write them next to the words. Which letters make no sound at all? _____ The sound you heard in Group 2 is the long vowel /e/, and it makes the sound of its own name, "e." For spelling, the long vowel /e/ can be represented by four combinations of letters—*e_e, ea, ee,* and *y.* You can use the clue word *easy* to help you remember the sound.

Each of the following words is missing a long vowel /e/ combination. Practice the long vowel /e/ combinations of *e_e, ee, ea,* and *y* by writing them in the blank spaces. Rewrite the whole word on the lines provided.

5. m _ _ ntime _____   **7.** potbell _ _____
6. str _ _ mline _____   **8.** k _ _ psake _____

In Group 3, the common letter is *i*. Can you hear the sound of the letter *i?* Break the words into sounds using slash marks and write them next to the words. Which letters make no sound at all? _____ The sound you heard in Group 3 is the long vowel /i/, and it makes the sound of its own name, "i." For spelling, the long vowel /i/ can be represented by four combinations of letters—*i_e, ie, igh,* and *y.* You can use the clue word *line* to help you remember the sound.

Each of the following words is missing a long vowel /i/ combination. Practice the long vowel /i/ combinations of *i_e, ie, igh,* and *y* by writing them in the blank spaces. Rewrite the whole word on the lines provided.

9. l _ f _ time _____

10. b _ laws _____

11. dayl _ _ _ t _____

12. d _ _ hard _____

In Group 4, the common letter is *o*. Can you hear the sound of the letter *o*? Break the words into sounds using slash marks and write them next to the words. Which letters make no sound at all? _____ The sound you heard in Group 4 is the long vowel /o/, and it makes the sound of its own name, "o." For spelling, the long vowel /o/ can be represented by four combinations of letters—*o_e, oe, ow,* and *oa*. You can use the clue word *toe* to help you remember the sound.

Each word below is missing a long vowel /o/ combination. Practice the long vowel /o/ combinations of *o_e, oe, ow,* and *oa* by writing them in the blank spaces. Rewrite the whole word on the lines provided.

13. h _ m_ work _____

14. downl _ _ d _____

15. st _ _ away _____

16. t _ _ nail _____

In Group 5, the common letter is *u*. Can you hear the sound of the letter *u*? Break the words into sounds using slash marks and write them next to the words. Which letters make no sound at all? _____ The sound you heard in Group 5 is the long vowel /u/, and it makes the sound of its own name, "u." For spelling, the long vowel /u/ can be represented by five combinations of letters—*u_e, ue, oo, ew,* and *ui*. You can use the clue word *blue* to help you remember the sound.

Each of the following words is missing a long vowel /u/ combination. Practice the long vowel /u/ combinations of *u_e, ue, oo, ew,* and *ui* by writing them in the blank spaces. Rewrite the word on the lines provided.

17. fr _ _ tcake _____

18. n _ _ spaper _____

19. aftern _ _ n _____

20. bl _ _ print _____

REFLECTION

What did you notice about the final letter *e* in each of the vowel combinations? _____

_____

What can you say about the second vowel in each vowel combination?

_____

How will the clue words help you?

_____

Why is it important to remember the letter combinations for the sound?

_____

In the long vowel combinations *a_e, e_e, i_e, o_e,* and *u_e,* the final *e* is silent. The second vowel in the vowel pairs *ai, ay, ee, ea, ie, oa, oe, ue, ui,* and *oo,* is also silent. Remember this rule:

If two vowels are a *pair*, the first vowel says its own name and the other vowel is usually silent.

There are many exceptions to the rule, including the word *diet.* There is a vowel pair in this word, but the rule does not apply because the word has two syllables. The first syllable is open and the vowel is a long sound. The second syllable has a vowel as the first letter, so the vowel also makes a sound. Written as two syllables, the word *diet* looks like this: *di-et.*

There are many words like this, but don't be discouraged—if you can remember the vowel pair rule, you're on your way to unlocking the secrets to becoming a great speller.

EXERCISE 3: PRACTICE WITH COMPOUND WORDS

Directions: Put a slash mark (/) between the two words that make up the compound word. The first one has been done for you.

1. home/ward
2. sunlight
3. rowboat
4. payday
5. keepsake

6. dewdrop
7. grapefruit
8. tollbooth
9. raindrop
10. seafood

EXERCISE 4: PRACTICE WRITING SPELLING LIST 3

Directions: Go back to Exercise 1. Look at the three words that are the same on each line. Write each of these words only once on the lines below. This would be a good time to have your study buddy dictate the words to you.

1. _____
2. _____
3. _____
4. _____
5. _____

6. _____
7. _____
8. _____
9. _____
10. _____

Consult your dictionary if the meaning of a word is unfamiliar to you.

Check your answers with the answer key at the end of this lesson.

My score for Exercise 4 is _____ out of 10.

EXERCISE 5: PRACTICE SPELLING LIST 3 IN CONTEXT

Directions: Use any word in Exercise 4 to complete each phrase. For added practice, rewrite the entire phrase in your own sentence on the provided line. The first one has been done for you.

1. food with a *homestyle* flavor

   Where can we order food with a homestyle flavor?

2. _____ and downsize the business

   _____

3. falling _____

   _____

4. banking on _____

   _____

5. a drifting _____ on a lake

   _____

6. a nesting _____

   _____

7. eating _____ for breakfast

   _____

8. warm, shimmering _____

   _____

9. a single _____ on a leaf

   _____

10. memories in a _____ box

   _____

Check your answers with the answer key at the end of this lesson. Only the words that go in the blanks are given, since everyone will create different sentences.

My score for Exercise 5 is _____ out of 10.

VARIATIONS

In some words the long /a/ sound is spelled with the letters *ey*, as in the clue word *they,* and *ei*, as in the clue word *eight*. The following is a list of other words in which *ey* and *ei* spell the sound of long /a/. Read the words aloud and circle the letter combinations in each word.

obey	hey	they
eight	weight	sleigh
heinous	neighbor	whey

In some words the long /e/ sound is spelled with the letters *ie*, as in the clue word *piece,* and *ei*, as in the clue word *receive*. The following is a list of other words in which *ie* and *ei* spell the sound of long /e/. Read the words aloud and circle the letter combinations in each word.

piece	niece	believe
relieve	relief	chief
leisure	seize	receipt
conceive	receive	neither

In some words the long /o/ sound is spelled with the letters *ou*, as in the clue word *dough*. The following is a list of other words in which *ou* spells the sound of long /o/. Read the words aloud and circle the letter combinations in each word.

dough	boulder	shoulder

The long /u/ sound is sometimes spelled with the letters *oo*. (See page 32 for long vowel /u/ combinations.) However, the letters *oo* do not always have the sound as in the word *food, cool, pool, smooth,* and *booth*. The letters *oo* represent another sound as in the word *cook*. Here is a list of other words that make the sound as in the word *cook*. Read the words aloud and circle the letter combinations that make that sound.

hook	book	took	look
crook	stood	wool	wood
hood	shook	woodpecker	

The following words contain the long vowel /o/. The letter *l* in these words signals that the *o* that precedes it will take the long vowel /o/ sound. Read each of the following words aloud and listen for the letter *o*.

Notice that it sounds like its own name. As you say each word, spell it on paper.

sold	bold	fold	gold
hold	cold	mold	scold

Practice writing these variations in your notebook. It's easier to remember them if you keep them in the same section of your notebook.

Do you want more challenging compound words with long vowel sounds? Try these! Call on your study buddy to dictate them to you as you write them in your notebook.

bookkeeper	overweight	weightlifter	overnight
oversight	keyboard	honeydew	honeysuckle
creditworthy	volleyball		

EXERCISE 6: WHAT HAVE YOU LEARNED?

Directions: Go back to Exercise 1. Look at the words that are the same on each line. Write these compound words only once on the following blank lines; then put a slash mark (/) between the two shorter words. Next to each word, write the letters that represent the sounds you hear. The first one has been done for you. Check your answers with the answer key at the end of this lesson.

1. home/style /h/o/m/s/t/i/l/
2. _____
3. _____
4. _____
5. _____
6. _____
7. _____
8. _____
9. _____
10. _____

11. What long vowel sound do you hear in the word *seasick*?

    _____

12. What long vowel sound do you hear in the word *wishbone*?

    _____

13. What long vowel sound do you hear in the word *capsize*?

    _____

14. What long vowel sound do you hear in the word *cornflakes*?

    _____

15. What long vowel sound do you hear in the word *fruitcake*?

    _____

Which word on each line is **not** a compound word? Circle it.

16. delete   peanut   teaspoon   meantime
17. manhole   compete   pigsty   wholesale
18. downsize   newspaper   database   athlete
19. wishbone   handshake   pleasure   snakebite
20. holiday   daytime   railroad   sunshine

Check your answers with the answer key at the end of this lesson.
My score for Exercise 6 is _____ out of 20.

ANSWER KEY FOR LESSON 3
Exercise 1

1. homework
2. bluebell
3. drewdrop
4. midnight
5. grapenuts
6. rowboats
7. playboy
8. rainfalls
9. knapsack
10. steamline

14. download
15. stowaway
16. toenail
17. fruitcake
18. newspaper
19. afternoon
20. blueprint

Exercise 2

1. dressmaker
2. stagecoach
3. payday
4. raindrop
5. meantime
6. streamline
7. potbelly
8. keepsake
9. lifetime
10. bylaws
11. daylight
12. diehard
13. homework

Exercise 3

1. home/ward
2. sun/light
3. row/boat
4. pay/day
5. keep/sake
6. dew/drop
7. grape/fruit
8. toll/booth
9. rain/drop
10. sea/food

Exercise 4

1. homestyle
2. bluejay
3. dewdrop
4. sunlight

5. grapefruit
6. rowboat
7. payday
8. raindrops
9. keepsake
10. streamline

Exercise 5

1. homestyle
2. streamline
3. raindrops
4. payday
5. rowboat
6. bluejay
7. grapefruit
8. sunlight
9. dewdrop
10. keepsake

Exercise 6

1. home/style /h/o/m/s/t/i/l/
2. blue/jay /b/l/u/j/a/
3. dew/drop /d/u/d/r/o/p/
4. sun/light /s/u/n/l/i/t/
5. grape/fruit /g/r/a/p/f/r/u/t/
6. row/boat /r/o/b/o/t/
7. pay/day /p/a/d/a/
8. rain/drops /r/a/n/d/r/o/p/s/
9. keep/sake /k/e/p/s/a/k/
10. stream/line /s/t/r/e/m/l/i/n/
11. long /e/
12. long /o/
13. long /i/
14. long /a/
15. long /u/, long /a/
16. delete
17. compete
18. athlete
19. pleasure
20. holiday

Barnes & Noble, Inc.
6111 sunrise blvd
citrus heights, ca 95610
916-853-1511 01-01-00 S02885 R005

Easy English: Basic Gram	12.95
1560521988	
Painless Grammar	8.95
0812097815	
You've Only Got Three Se	4.98
0641015550	
Practical Spelling: The	13.95
1576850838	
The Writing Road to Read	17.95
0688100074	
1100 Words You Need to K	10.95
0812016203	

SUB TOTAL	69.73
SALES TAX	5.40
TOTAL	75.13
AMOUNT TENDERED	
CASH	75.13

TOTAL PAYMENT	80.13
CHANGE	5.00

Thanks for shopping at Barnes & Noble!
#46670 01-01-00 01:22P J.T.

Bookseller Since 1873

this receipt within 30 days.

If you are not satisfied with your
purchase for any reason you may return
it in salable condition accompanied by
this receipt within 30 days.

If you are not satisfied with your
purchase for any reason you may return
it in salable condition accompanied by
this receipt within 30 days.

LESSON | 4

PAIRING VOWELS

In Lessons 2 and 3, you learned to spell compound words with long and short vowel sounds, and were introduced to the letter/sound relationship method. In this lesson, you will meet pairs of vowels that have a unique sound and continue to use the letter/sound relationship method. When you use these skills, more and more words will become easier for you to spell.

EXERCISE 1: EYEBALLING SPELLING LIST 4

Directions: Sweep your eyes across the line from left to right and back again. Do it quickly. Circle the word in each line that looks different from the others on that line.

Are you ready? Get set . . . Go!

1. pointers	pointers	pointers	painters
2. poise	pose	poise	poise
3. person	poison	poison	poison
4. boycott	boycott	buoyant	boycott
5. oysters	oysters	oilers	oysters
6. bouncers	bouncers	bounces	bouncers
7. county	county	county	country

8. crowd	crowd	crowed	crowd
9. prawns	pawns	pawns	pawns
10. automatic	automotive	automatic	automatic

Check your answers with the answer key at the end of this lesson. **My score for Exercise 1 is _____ out of 10.**

REFLECTION

Go back to the words that are the **same** on each line in Exercise 1. Find the vowel in each word. Do you notice anything about them? _____

_____

If you said that the words have pairs of vowels like *oi, oy, ou, ow, au,* and *aw* (*aw* and *ow* are exceptions because the letter *w* is not a vowel) in them, then you have a very keen eye. Go back and put a circle around the pairs of vowels.

Move on to Exercise 2, Sound Inventory, to hear the sounds of the vowel pairs in this lesson.

EXERCISE 2: SOUND INVENTORY

Directions: Listen to yourself as you read each group of words aloud. **You must read the words out loud**. There's something that the letters and sounds in each group have in common. Put a circle around the vowel combinations that are the same, and then write those vowel combinations on the lines provided.

GROUP 1

joy	voice
ploy	moist
oyster	point

GROUP 2

out	cow
blouse	owl
ounce	wow

GROUP 3

taunt	dawn
August	awning
faucet	hawk

_____ _____   _____ _____   _____ _____

In Group 1, the common letters are *oy* and *oi*. Can you hear the sound? If you need help, break the words up into sounds using slash marks. The word *joy* should look like /j/oy/ and *voice* should look like /v/oi/s/. (The letter *c* has an /s/ sound.) Now can you hear the sound? It has the same sound found in the clue phrase *Joy's voice*. The difficulty with this sound is knowing when to use *oi* and when to use *oy*. As a general rule, *oy* is written at the beginning or the end of a word and *oi* is written in the middle of the word. The common exception to the rule is the word *oil*.

In Group 2, the common letters are *ou* and *ow*. Can you hear the sound? If you need help, use slash marks to break up the words. The word *wow* should look like /w/ow/ and *cloud* should look like /c/l/ou/d/. Now can you hear the sound? It has the same sound found in the clue phrase *Wow what a cloud!* The difficulty with this sound is knowing when to use *ou* or *ow*. There's no rule to follow in this case. The only hint is that *ou* at the end of a word looks awkward, so *ow* is usually used. See the Challenge section in this lesson for some *ou* and *ow* words you can practice.

In Group 3, the common letters are *au* and *aw*. Can you hear the sound? If you need help, break the words *taunt* and *hawk* into sounds. The word *taunt* should look like /t/au/n/t/ and *hawk* should look like /h/aw/k/. Now do you hear the sound? It has the same sound found in the clue phrase *taunting hawk*. The difficulty with this sound is knowing when to use *au* or *aw*. The only hint is that *au* at the end of a word looks awkward, so *aw* is usually used.

REFLECTION

What pairs of vowels did you learn in this lesson? _____

How will the clue words help you? _____
_____

Why is it important to remember the letter combinations for the sound?
_____
_____

If you remember the sounds covered in this lesson as well as the letters for those sounds, you have another way to widen your pool of spelling words. Spelling is a relationship between letters and sounds, and the next exercise helps you understand this relationship.

EXERCISE 3: PRACTICE WITH LETTER COMBINATIONS AND SOUNDS

Directions: Use the clue words to remind you of the letter/sound relationship. In each space, write the letter combinations from Exercise 2 to correctly spell each word.

1. h _ _ k   6. cl _ _ d   11. v _ _ ce
2. s _ _ ce   7. gr _ _ nd   12. b _ _ cott
3. f _ _ cet   8. ar _ _ se   13. dec _ _
4. _ _ tomatic   9. tr _ _ t   14. m _ _ st
5. p _ _ per   10. cr _ _ n   15. l _ _ alty

Check your answers with the answer key at the end of the lesson.

My score for Exercise 3 is _____ out of 15.

EXERCISE 4: PRACTICE WRITING SPELLING LIST 4

Directions: Go back to Exercise 1. Look at the three words that are the same on each line. Write each of these words only once on the lines below. This would be a good time to have your study buddy dictate the words to you.

1. _____   6. _____
2. _____   7. _____
3. _____   8. _____
4. _____   9. _____
5. _____   10. _____

Consult your dictionary if the meaning of a word is unfamiliar to you.

Check your answers with the answer key at the end of this lesson.

My score for Exercise 4 is _____ out of 10.

EXERCISE 5: PRACTICE WRITING SPELLING LIST 4 IN CONTEXT

Directions: Use any word in Exercise 4 to complete each phrase. For added practice, rewrite the entire phrase in your own sentence on the provided line.

1. an _____ coffee maker

   _____

2. rat _____

   _____

3. _____ on a half shell

   _____

4. _____ and grace of a model

   _____

5. _____ at the club

_____

6. a citywide _____

_____

7. The _____ clerk's office

_____

8. _____ with rubber tips

_____

9. _____ all the gold jewelry

_____

10. a _____ at the bus stop

_____

Check your answers with the answer key at the end of this lesson. Only the words that go in the blanks are given, since everyone will create different sentences.

My score for Exercise 5 is _____ out of 10.

VARIATIONS

Sometimes when *a* precedes *l*, as in the words below, the *a* takes on the /aw/ sound. Read each of the following words aloud and notice that the sound /aw/l/ can be spelled either *al* or *all*. Circle these letters in each word.

almost	always	already	walnut
halter	chalk	salt	stall
hallway	mall	fallen	small

The letters *ou* are used to spell other sounds, but they are not as frequent. Read each word aloud to listen for the sound of the letters *ou* in this group. Do you hear the **long /o/** as found in the clue word *home?*

thor**ou**gh	sh**ou**lder	b**ou**lder
d**ou**gh	th**ou**gh	p**ou**ltry

The letters *ou* in these words make the **short /u/** sound, as found in the clue word *up.*

r**ou**gh	t**ou**gh	en**ou**gh	y**ou**ng
c**ou**ple	d**ou**ble	tr**ou**ble	c**ou**ntry

The letters *ou* in these words make a **long /u/** sound, as found in the clue word *fruit*.

through   youth   group   soup

Practice writing these variations in your notebook.

Do you want more challenging words? Try these! Call on your study buddy to dictate them to you as you write them in your notebook.

automatically	authority	August	auditorium
sawdust	applause	exhaust	awkward
installation	waltz	alteration	although
almost	altogether	already	scald
router	southbound	foundling	compound
employment	annoyance	enjoyment	royalty
rejoice	cloister	boisterous	moisture

EXERCISE 6: WHAT HAVE YOU LEARNED?

Circle the word on each line that does **not** have the sound found in the clue phrase *taunting hawk.*

1. straws   drawer   downing   dawning
2. lawn   claws   clowns   bawl

Circle the word on each line that does **not** have the sound found in the clue phrase *Joy's voice.*

3. hoists   host   spoilers   destroyers
4. boilers   broilers   employ   noses
5. coil   cool   choices   avoids

Circle the word on each line that does **not** have the sound found in the clue phrase *Wow what a cloud!*

6. housewares   fountains   mountains   fortune
7. shots   shouts   slouch   grouch
8. bounty   beauty   scouts   grounded

The review exercises in this book (usually Exercise 6) help you practice the letter/sound relationship method. Since knowing compound words can greatly enhance your spelling power, they are reviewed frequently throughout this book.

Which word is **not** a compound word? Circle it.

9. mountainside   downtown   boyfriend   noisy

10. cloudburst   however   lawyer   lawnmower

Check your answers with the answer key at the end of this lesson.

My score for Exercise 6 is _____ out of 10.

ANSWER KEY FOR LESSON 4

Exercise 1

1. painters
2. pose
3. person
4. buoyant
5. oilers
6. bounces
7. country
8. crowed
9. prawns
10. automotive

11. voice
12. boycott
13. decoy
14. moist
15. loyalty

Exercise 4

1. pointers
2. poise
3. poison
4. boycott
5. oysters
6. bouncers
7. county
8. crowd
9. pawns
10. automatic

Exercise 3

1. hawk
2. sauce
3. faucet
4. automatic
5. pauper
6. cloud
7. ground
8. arouse
9. trout
10. crown

Exercise 5

1. automatic
2. poison
3. oysters

4. poise
5. bouncers
6. boycott
7. county
8. pointers
9. pawns
10. crowd

Exercise 6

1. downing
2. clowns
3. host
4. noses
5. cool
6. fortune
7. shots
8. beauty
9. noisy
10. lawyer

LESSON | 5

There are still more vowel combinations to learn. This lesson introduces you to vowels that have a controlling partner. The vowel-consonant combination you'll learn about in this lesson makes a sound commonly called a *murmur* sound.

WHAT'S ALL THE MURMURING ABOUT?

EXERCISE 1: EYEBALLING SPELLING LIST 5

Directions: Sweep your eyes across the line from left to right and back again. Do it quickly. Circle the word in each line that looks different from the others on that line.

Are you ready? Get set . . . Go!

1. bartend	bartend	barter	bartend
2. carton	cartoon	cartoon	cartoon
3. market	market	market	marker
4. carnivals	cardinals	carnivals	carnivals
5. cargo	carton	cargo	cargo
6. glory	glory	golly	glory
7. happen	harpoon	harpoon	harpoon

47

8. mortar	mortar	motor	mortar
9. stormy	stormy	stormy	stony
10. organ	organ	order	organ

Check your answers with the answer key at the end of this lesson. **My score for Exercise 1 is _____ out of 10.**

REFLECTION

Go back to the words that are the **same** on each line in Exercise 1. Find the **first** vowel in each word. Circle it. What letter is to the right of the **first** vowel? Circle that letter too. What can you say about these letter combinations? _____

_____

If you said that the letter *r* is next to the vowel, that's absolutely correct. Good for you! The vowels covered in Lessons 5 and 6 are controlled by the letter *r*. These letter combinations have unique sounds all their own. Move on to Exercise 2, Sound Inventory, to hear the sounds of this lesson.

EXERCISE 2: SOUND INVENTORY

Directions: Listen to yourself as you read each group of words aloud. **You must read the words out loud.** There's something that the letters and sounds in each group have in common. Put a circle around the letters that are the same, and then write them on the lines provided.

GROUP 1		GROUP 2	
art	tar	for	torn
ark	tart	form	born
cart	dark	fork	dorm
hard	park	corn	pork
_____	_____		

In Group 1, the common letters are *ar*. Can you hear the unique sound of /ar/? If you need help, break the words into sounds using slash marks. The word *cart* should be written as /c/ar/t/. Now can you hear the sound? It has the same beginning sound as found in the clue word *artist*.

In Group 2, the common letters are *or*. Can you hear the unique sound of /or/? If you need help, break the word into sounds using slash marks.

The word *pork* should be written as /p/or/k/. Now can you hear the sound? It has the same sound as the beginning sound in the clue word *orbit*.

The sounds of /ar/ and /or/ belong to a special group of vowels called **murmur vowels.** The letter *r* is the vowel's partner. The vowel combined with the letter *r* makes a unique sound.

REFLECTION

How will the clue words help you? _____

Why is it important to remember the letter combinations for the sound? _____

_____

What letter is the vowel's partner? ____

Why do you think these vowels are called murmur vowels?

_____

_____

If you remember the sounds covered so far as well as the letters for those sounds, you have more ways to widen your pool of spelling words. Always keep in mind that spelling is a relationship between letters and sounds. The vowels in this lesson have unique sounds because of their relationship with the letter *r*. In this relationship, the vowel is **controlled** by the letter *r*. All vowels that have the letter *r* as a partner are called **murmur vowels.** They have a completely different sound than the short or long vowels you met in Lessons 2 and 3.

The next exercise will help you remember these letters and sounds.

EXERCISE 3: PRACTICE WITH LETTER COMBINATIONS AND SOUNDS

Directions: Use the clue word *artist* to remind you of the letter/sound relationship. In each space, write the letter combinations to correctly spell each word. Read each group of words aloud to help you understand the letter/sound relationship.

1. h _ _vest	**5.** sp _ _ kle	**9.** enl _ _ ge	**13.** _ _ my
2. h _ _ poon	**6.** c _ _ go	**10.** m _ _ vel	**14.** rem _ _ k
3. p _ _ tner	**7.** reg _ _ d	**11.** st _ _ ve	**15.** t _ _ get
4. p _ _ don	**8.** al _ _ m	**12.** _ _ gue	

Directions: Use the clue word *orbit* to remind you of the letter/sound relationship. In each space, write the letter combinations to correctly spell each word. Read each group of words aloud to help you understand the letter/sound relationship.

16. arm _ _   **20.** _ _ chid   **24.** rep _ _ t   **28.** f _ _ mula
17. _ _ al   **21.** t _ _ nado   **25.** dep _ _ t   **29.** f _ _ titude
18. _ _ dain   **22.** t _ _ rent   **26.** n _ _ th   **30.** d _ _ mit _ _ y
19. _ _ ate   **23.** p _ _ t   **27.** h _ _ net

How many of these words can you spell on your own? Give it a try.

Check your answers with the answer key at the end of this lesson.

My score for Exercise 3 is _____ out of 30.

EXERCISE 4: PRACTICE WRITING SPELLING LIST 5

Directions: Go back to Exercise 1. Look at the three words that are the same on each line. Write each of these words only once on the lines below. This would be a good time to have your study buddy dictate the words to you.

1. _____   **6.** _____
2. _____   **7.** _____
3. _____   **8.** _____
4. _____   **9.** _____
5. _____   **10.** _____

Consult your dictionary if the meaning of a word is unfamiliar to you.

Check your answers with the answer key at the end of this lesson.

My score for Exercise 4 is _____ out of 10.

EXERCISE 5: PRACTICE WRITING SPELLING LIST 5 IN CONTEXT

Directions: Use any word in Exercise 4 to complete each phrase. For added practice, rewrite the entire phrase in your own sentence on the provided line.

1. _____ weather

_____

2. artistic _____ characters

_____

3. _____ at harvest time

_____

4. loading _____ onto the ships

_____

5. bring the fruits to _____

_____

6. _____ at club "ORBIT"

_____

7. waving the flag in all its _____

_____

8. whaling with a _____

_____

9. hardened _____ between the tiles

_____

10. orchestrated _____ music

_____

Check your answers with the answer key at the end of this lesson. Only the words that go in the blanks are given, since everyone will create different sentences.

My score for Exercise 5 is _____ out of 10.

VARIATIONS

In some words, the /or/ sound is spelled *ore*, *oor*, or *our*, as in the clue words *core*, *poor*, and *mourn*. Read each of the following words **aloud** and circle the letters that make the /or/ sound.

score	store	implore	doorway
floor	snore	swore	spore
more	mourn	gore	lore

Practice writing these variations in your notebook.

Do you want more challenging words with the /ar/ and /or/ sounds? Try these! Call on your study buddy to dictate them to you as you write them in your notebook.

discharge	armory	article	departure
compartment	remarkable	regardless	transportation
fortitude	torrential	orchestra	normal
export	dormitory	organist	

EXERCISE 6: WHAT HAVE YOU LEARNED?

Directions: First read each sentence aloud. Then go back to the sentence and circle the words that have the same sound as found in the clue word *artist*. This is a good time to have your study buddy dictate the sentences to you.

1. The newspaper article was titled "The Garbage Barge Harvest."
2. The participants were discharged early in March.
3. The charcoal sparkled in the evening darkness.

Directions: First read each sentence aloud. Then go back to the sentence and circle the words that have the same sound as found in the clue word *orbit*. This is a good time to have your study buddy dictate the sentences to you.

4. The orchestra presented works that were far from ordinary.
5. The immigrants with expired green cards were deported on the cargo ship.
6. The oral report on the lifestyle of an organ transplant recipient was quite informative.

Which of the following words are not compound words? Circle them.

7. vineyard   cardboard   hardship   ornament
8. enlargement   cornbread   yardstick   barbell
9. hardwood   dormitory   parkway   barnyard
10. carnation   hardship   sweetheart   carpetbagger

Check your answers with the answer key at the end of this lesson.
My score for Exercise 6 is _____ out of 10.

ANSWER KEY FOR LESSON 5

Exercise 1
1. barter
2. carton
3. marker
4. cardinals
5. carton
6. golly
7. happen
8. motor
9. stony
10. order

Exercise 3
1. harvest
2. harpoon
3. partner
4. pardon
5. sparkle
6. cargo
7. regard
8. alarm
9. enlarge
10. marvel
11. starve
12. argue
13. army
14. remark
15. target
16. armor
17. oral
18. ordain
19. orate
20. orchid
21. tornado
22. torrent
23. port
24. report
25. deport
26. north
27. hornet
28. formula
29. fortitude
30. dormitory

Exercise 4
1. bartend
2. cartoon
3. market
4. carnivals
5. cargo
6. glory
7. harpoon
8. mortar
9. stormy
10. organ

Exercise 5
1. stormy
2. cartoon
3. carnivals
4. cargo
5. market
6. bartend
7. glory
8. harpoon
9. mortar
10. organ

Exercise 6

1. article, Garbage, Barge, Harvest
2. participants, discharged, March
3. charcoal, sparkled, darkness
4. orchestra, ordinary (There's no mistake, the word *work* is not included. To be sure, say the word aloud and listen for the sound of the letters *or*.)
5. deported
6. oral, report, organ, informative
7. ornament
8. enlargement
9. dormitory
10. carnation

LESSON | 6

The murmurs continue in this lesson. The letter *r* is busy controlling the sounds of the vowels it's paired with. Spelling should become easier as you continue to apply the letter/sound relationship method to the many words you will meet in this lesson.

THE MURMURS CONTINUE

EXERCISE 1: EYEBALLING SPELLING LIST 6

Directions: Sweep your eyes across the line from left to right and back again. Do it quickly. Circle the word in each line that looks different from the others on that line.

Are you ready? Get set . . . Go!

1. certain	curtain	curtain	curtain
2. furnishes	furnishes	furnishes	finishes
3. termites	terminates	terminates	terminates
4. vertical	vertical	virtual	vertical
5. persist	permit	permit	permit
6. conserve	conserve	converse	conserve
7. birch	birth	birth	birth

8. curve	carve	curve	curve
9. thirsty	thirsty	thirty	thirsty
10. fertile	fertile	fertile	futile

Check your answers with the answer key at the end of this lesson. **My score for Exercise 1 is _____ out of 10.**

REFLECTION

Go back to the words that are the **same** on each line in Exercise 1. Find the **first** vowel in each word. Circle it. What letter is to the right of the vowel? _____ Circle that letter too. What can you say about these letter combinations? _____

_____

If you said that the letter *r* is next to the **first** vowel, that's correct. In this lesson, the vowels *e, i,* and *u* are controlled by the letter *r*. These letter combinations have one sound, though it can be spelled *er, ir,* and *ur*. Move on to Exercise 2, Sound Inventory, to hear the sound of this lesson.

EXERCISE 2: SOUND INVENTORY

Directions: Listen to yourself as you read each group of words aloud. **You must read the words out loud.** There's something that the letters and sounds in each group have in common. Put a circle around the letters that are the same in each group and then write the two letters on the lines provided.

GROUP 1		**GROUP 2**		**GROUP 3**	
her	term	dirt	bird	fur	turn
herd	clerk	sir	stir	surf	curl
verse	fern	skirt	flirt	burn	burst
_____		_____		_____	

In Group 1, the common letters are *er*. Can you hear the sound of the letters *er*? The *e* doesn't make it's usual sound—the one you hear in the word *egg*. In fact, you can't separate the sounds of the two letters, because *e* and *r* combine to form **one** sound. If you need help hearing this sound, use slash marks to break up the words. The word *her* should be written as /h/er/ and the word *clerk* should be written as /c/l/er/k/. Now can you hear the sound? It has the same sound as found in the clue word *nervous*.

In Group 2, the common letters are *ir*. Can you hear the sound of the letters *ir*? If you need help, use slash marks to break the words into sounds. Notice again that one sound is represented by two letters. The word *sir* should be written as /s/ir/ and the word *stir* should be written as /s/t/ir/. Now can you hear the sound? It has the same sound as found in the clue word *dirty*.

In Group 3, the common letters are *ur*. Can you hear the sound of the letters *ur*? If you need help, use slash marks to break the words into sounds. The word *fur* should be written as /f/ur/ and the word *turn* should be written as /t/ur/n/. Now can you hear the sound? It has the same sound as found in the clue word *burglar*.

REFLECTION

Say *fur, sir,* and *her*. By now you must agree that all three words have the same sound. But there's an obvious difference between the words. What is the difference? _____

_____

If you said that they have the same sound but use different letters to represent the /er/ sound, you're absolutely correct. The difficult part of this sound is that there's no set rule for when to use the letters *er, ir,* or *ur*. Use the clue phrase *nervous, dirty burglar* to help you remember that the /er/ sound is spelled *er, ir,* or *ur*.

Move on to the next exercise to help you remember the letters that make the sound in this lesson.

EXERCISE 3: PRACTICE WITH LETTER COMBINATIONS AND SOUNDS

Directions: Use the clue phrase **nervous, dirty burglar** to remind you of the letter/sound relationship. In each space, write the letter combinations to correctly spell each word.

nervous	dirty	burglar
1. f _ _ tile	11. b _ _ th	21. _ _ ge
2. v _ _ tical	12. wh _ _ ling	22. _ _ gent
3. p _ _ mit	13. c _ _ cle	23. b _ _ den
4. cons _ _ ve	14. th _ _ teen	24. b _ _ st
5. t _ _ minate	15. th _ _ sty	25. c _ _ ved
6. c _ _ tain	16. th _ _ ty	26. f _ _ nish
7. s _ _ mon	17. c _ _ cus	27. g _ _ gle
8. rev _ _ se	18. v _ _ tual	28. c _ _ tain
9. n _ _ vous	19. fl _ _ t	29. t _ _ nips
10. m _ _ ge	20. enc _ _ cle	30. j _ _ y

Read each group of words aloud. This will help to reinforce the letter/sound relationship for you.

How many of these words can you spell on your own? This would be a good time to have your study buddy dictate the words to you.

Using Letter/Sound Relationships

As you write the words, say the sounds in the word and think of the letters that make the sounds. By now you should be using the correct letters that make the sound. If you're doing it right, you're on your way to becoming a great speller.

EXERCISE 4: PRACTICE WRITING SPELLING LIST 6

Directions: Go back to Exercise 1. Look at the three words that are the same on each line. Write each of these words only once on the lines below. This would be a good time to have your study buddy dictate the words to you.

1. _____   6. _____

2. _____   7. _____

3. _____   8. _____

4. _____   9. _____

5. _____   10. _____

Consult your dictionary if the meaning of a word is unfamiliar to you.

Check your answers with the answer key at the end of this lesson.

My score for Exercise 4 is _____ out of 10.

EXERCISE 5: PRACTICE WRITING SPELLING LIST 6 IN CONTEXT.

Directions: Use any word in Exercise 4 to complete each phrase. For added practice, rewrite the entire phrase in your own sentence on the provided line.

1. a _____ on a window

_____

2. _____ farmland

_____

3. _____ energy

_____

4. a dangerous _____ on a parkway

_____

5. _____ lines

_____

6. _____ of a newborn

_____

7. _____ employment

_____

8. _____ an apartment

_____

9. _____ ballplayers need a drink

_____

10. a driver's _____

_____

Check your answers with the answer key at the end of this lesson. Only the words that go in the blanks are given, since everyone will create different sentences.

My score for Exercise 5 is _____ out of 10.

VARIATIONS

In some words, the /er/ sound is written with the letters *or*, as in the word *work*. Read each word aloud and circle the letters *or* in each word. Practice writing these words in your notebook.

work	word	worth	worry
color	worship	worm	worse
world	attorney		

The following letter combinations are also controlled by the letter *r*. However, these combinations aren't as frequent, and the sound they produce is different.

air**port**	h**air**	f**air**	d**are**
c**are**	b**are**	th**ere**	wh**ere**
th**eir**	h**eir**	w**ear**	b**ear**

Practice writing these variations in your notebook.

Do you want more challenging words that use the /er/ sound? Try these! Call on your study buddy to dictate them to you as you write them in your notebook.

internship	personal	personnel	customer
salesperson	compressor	memory	worldwide
worthwhile	workshop		

EXERCISE 6: WHAT HAVE YOU LEARNED?

The /ur/, /ir/, and /er/ sounds in this lesson, and the /ar/ and /or/ sounds in Lesson 5 are called **murmur vowels.** All of these vowels are controlled by the letter *r* and make a unique sound. Write all the words in the following sentences that have murmur vowels in your notebook. This is a good time to have your study buddy dictate the sentences to you.

1. The torrential rains dumped thirty inches of water into the fertile valley.
2. Thirty gorgeous mermaids surrounded the surfer in the turquoise waters of Bermuda.
3. Snorkeling and surfing are adventurous water sports.
4. The German circus performers whirled on the flying trapeze.
5. The dirty water percolated through the special filters.
6. The storybook characters will be impersonated by the professional actors.
7. The patient's epidermis was destroyed by second degree burns and the surgeon performed skin grafting.
8. Please verify the merger between the two partners.
9. There was still a murmur in the audience after the curtain opened.
10. The morning sermon reflected life in the desert in ancient times.

Check your answers with the answer key at the end of this lesson.

My score for Exercise 6 is _____ out of 10.

ANSWER KEY FOR LESSON 6

Exercise 1

1. certain
2. finishes
3. termites
4. virtual
5. persist
6. converse
7. birch
8. carve
9. thirty
10. futile

Exercise 3

1. fertile
2. vertical
3. permit
4. conserve
5. terminate
6. certain
7. sermon
8. reverse
9. nervous
10. merge
11. birth
12. whirling
13. circle
14. thirteen
15. thirsty
16. thirty
17. circus
18. virtual
19. flirt
20. encircle
21. urge
22. urgent
23. burden
24. burst
25. curved
26. furnish
27. gurgle
28. curtain
29. turnips
30. jury

Exercise 4

1. curtain
2. furnishes
3. terminates
4. vertical
5. permit
6. conserve
7. birth
8. curve
9. thirsty
10. fertile

Exercise 5

1. curtain
2. fertile
3. conserve
4. curve
5. vertical, curved
6. birth
7. terminates
8. furnishes
9. thirsty
10. permit

Exercise 6

1. torrential, thirty, water, fertile
2. thirty, gorgeous, mermaids, surrounded, surfer, turquoise, waters, Bermuda
3. snorkeling, surfing, adventurous, water, sports
4. German, circus, performers, whirled
5. dirty, water, percolated, filters
6. storybook, characters, impersonated, actors
7. epidermis, burns, surgeon, performed
8. verify, merger, partners
9. murmur, after, curtain
10. morning, sermon, desert

LESSON | 7

In this lesson, you will learn that two consonants can make one sound. These are called **consonant pairs**. You will also make letter/sound changes in words. This is called **substitution**. This substitution strategy will help you greatly expand your pool of spelling words.

WHAT A PAIR!

EXERCISE 1: EYEBALLING SPELLING LIST 7

Directions: Sweep your eyes across the line from left to right and back again. Do it quickly. Circle the word in each line that looks different from the others on that line.

Are you ready? Get set . . . Go!

1. charmer	charmer	charmer	churner
2. style	stylish	stylish	stylish
3. shorten	shorter	shorten	shorten
4. shameful	shameful	shameful	spiteful
5. starchy	stormy	starchy	starchy
6. charter	charter	charter	chanter
7. shiver	shiver	sliver	shiver

8. cherish	perish	cherish	cherish
9. brunch	brunch	brush	brunch
10. ashes	ushers	ushers	ushers

Check your answers with the answer key at the end of this lesson. **My score for Exercise 1 is _____ out of 10.**

REFLECTION

Go back to the words that are the **same** on each line in Exercise 1. Look for the letter combinations *sh* and *ch*. Circle each pair. For example, in the word *charmer,* you would circle the letters *ch*. After you circle the pairs of letters, think about where in the word the letters are located. What can you say about the locations of *sh* and *ch?* _____

_____

If you said that the letters *sh* and *ch* are located in three places, you're right. They can be written in the beginning, middle (meaning a place other than the beginning or end), and end of a word. Each of these pairs of letters makes a particular sound.

Move on to Exercise 2, Sound Inventory, to hear the sounds of this lesson.

EXERCISE 2: SOUND INVENTORY

Directions: Listen to yourself as you read each group of words aloud. **You must read the words out loud.** There is something that the letters and sounds in each group have in common. Put a circle around the letters that are the same in each group. Next, notice the **location** of these letters. Are they located in the **beginning, middle,** or **end?**

GROUP 1

shy	rush	ashes
shelf	brush	ashamed
shine	leash	membership
short	cash	

GROUP 2

chew	each	peachy
chop	arch	enchantment
chart	lunch	preacher
chime	coach	teacher

In Group 1, the common letters are *sh*. Can you hear the sound of the letters *sh?* If you need help, use slash marks to break the words into sounds. The word *shy* should be written as /sh/y/ and the word *brush* should be written as /b/r/u/sh/. Now can you hear the sound? It has the same sound as found in the clue word *shake*. As you can see, the letters *sh* can appear anywhere in the word.

In Group 2, the common letters are *ch*. Can you hear the sound of the letters *ch*? If you need help, use slash marks to break the words into sounds. The word *chew* should be written as /ch/u/ and the word *chart* should be written as /ch/ar/t/. Now can you hear the sound? It has the same sound as the clue word *lunch*.

It's a good idea to go through all the words in both groups and break them into sounds using slash marks. There are many words there to help you review the sounds you've learned in Lessons 1–6.

REFLECTION

Say *shop* and *chop* aloud. By now you realize these pairs of letters have a special relationship. In each consonant pair, there are two letters. But how many sounds does each pair make? _____ How are the **consonant pairs** different from the **consonant blends**? _____

_____

_____

If you said that each pair of letters makes one sound, you're absolutely right! If you return to the Letter/Sound Relationship Key in the introduction, you will see that a consonant blend is two letters side-by-side, each with its own sound. The word *clamp* begins with the consonant blend represented by the letters *c* and *l*. You can hear both the letter *c* and the letter *l*. The same holds true for the word *stamp*. The letters *s* and *t* form a consonant blend. Each letter represents a sound. The word *champ*, however, begins with a consonant pair represented by the letters *ch*. The letters *c* and *h* do **not** each make their own sound. They are a pair of letters with one sound.

Move on to Exercise 3 to practice a substitution exercise. This kind of substitution will give you more spelling power.

EXERCISE 3: PRACTICE WITH SUBSTITUTION

Directions: Change the **first** consonant or the blend (two consonants) to one of the consonant pairs you learned in this lesson. This is the substitution strategy that will help you see connections between different words. Use the clue words *shake* and *lunch* to help you remember the letter/sound pair. Write the new word beside the old one on the provided line. The first three words are done for you.

1. made	_shade_	**11.** range	_____
2. hallow	_shallow_	**12.** wild	_____
3. farmer	_charmer_	**13.** telling	_____
4. liver	_____	**14.** perish	_____
5. game	_____	**15.** slimmer	_____
6. hilly	_____	**16.** sliver	_____
7. brat	_____	**17.** lift	_____
8. brew	_____	**18.** scout	_____
9. cop	_____	**19.** poke	_____
10. burn	_____	**20.** by	_____

Check your answers with the answer key at the end of this lesson.

Practice Hint

As you write the words, say the sounds in the word and think of the letters that make the sounds. By now you should be using the correct letters that make the sound. If you're doing it right, you're on your way to becoming a great speller.

Directions: Now use the same substitution strategy to make changes to the consonant at the **end** of the word. Write the new word on the provided line. The first three are done for you.

21. dam	_dash_	**31.** run	_____
22. mat	_mash_	**32.** can	_____
23. team	_teach_	**33.** rear	_____
24. at	_____	**34.** mug	_____
25. gum	_____	**35.** churn	_____
26. cram	_____	**36.** mart	_____
27. start	_____	**37.** clam	_____
28. perk	_____	**38.** torn	_____
29. flag	_____	**39.** pork	_____
30. rim	_____	**40.** fig	_____

Check your answers with the answer key at the end of this lesson.
My score for Exercise 3 is _____ out of 40.

EXERCISE 4: PRACTICE WRITING SPELLING LIST 7

Directions: Go back to Exercise 1. Look at the three words that are the same on each line. Write each of these words only once on the lines below. This would be a good time to have your study buddy dictate the words to you.

1. _____   6. _____
2. _____   7. _____
3. _____   8. _____
4. _____   9. _____
5. _____   10. _____

Consult your dictionary if the meaning of a word is unfamiliar to you.

Check your answers with the answer key at the end of this lesson.

My score for Exercise 4 is _____ out of 10.

EXERCISE 5: PRACTICE WRITING SPELLING LIST 7 IN CONTEXT

Directions: Use any word from Exercise 1 to complete each phrase. For added practice, rewrite the entire phrase in your own sentence on the provided line.

1. _____ clothing

_____

2. _____ in the theater

_____

3. a _____ act

_____

4. _____ with fear

_____

5. snake _____

_____

6. _____ foods

_____

7. _____ by three inches

_____

8. signed _____

_____

9. _____ at a restaurant

_____

10. _____ your love

_____

Check your answers with the answer key at the end of this lesson. Only the words that go in the blanks are given, since everyone will create different sentences.

My score for Exercise 5 is _____ out of 10.

VARIATIONS

In some words, the sound /ch/ at the end of the word is spelled *tch*, as in the word *patch.* The letter *t* is silent. Practice spelling the following words that contain this /ch/ variation. Circle the letters *tch* in each word, and then write the whole word in your notebook.

batch	hatch	latch	match
catch	witch	stitch	watch
scratch	hitch	pitch	ditch
switch	hutch	Dutch	sketch
fetch	snitch		

The letters *ch* also can be used to indicate the sound found in the first sound of the word **key.** Say each of the following words aloud. Circle the letters *ch* in each word and listen for the sound of /k/.

Christian	Christmas	chemical
scheduled	cholesterol	chorus

The letters *ch* also have the sound found in the first sound in the word **shake.** Say each of the following words aloud. Circle the letters *ch* in each word and listen for the sound of /sh/.

chic	chef	chenille
brochure	chivalry	

For added practice, write these words in your notebook and spell them out loud for your study buddy.

Do you want more challenging words that contain the letters *ch?* Try these! Call on your study buddy to dictate them to you as you write them in your notebook.

chromosome   chemotherapy   cholera   chamois

EXERCISE 6: WHAT HAVE YOU LEARNED?

Directions: Write a slash mark to separate the compound words, and then circle the consonant pairs *sh* or *ch* in each word.

1. chairman
2. shipyard
3. shellfish
4. stopwatch
5. sunshine
6. matchmaker
7. watchman
8. shutout
9. stopwatch
10. chalkboard
11. cheerleader
12. sheepskin
13. shoestring
14. shorthand
15. seashell
16. touchdown
17. hitchhike
18. latchkey
19. chambermaid
20. shutdown

Check your answers with the answer key at the end of this lesson.
My score for Exercise 6 is _____ out of 20.

ANSWER KEY FOR LESSON 7

Exercise 1
1. churner
2. style
3. shorter
4. spiteful
5. stormy
6. chanter
7. sliver
8. perish
9. brush
10. ashes

Exercise 3
1. shade
2. shallow
3. charmer
4. shiver
5. shame
6. chilly
7. chat
8. chew
9. shop, chop
10. churn
11. change
12. child
13. shelling

14. cherish
15. shimmer
16. shiver
17. shift
18. shout
19. choke
20. shy
21. dash
22. mash
23. teach
24. ash
25. gush
26. crash
27. starch
28. perch
29. flash
30. rich
31. rush
32. cash
33. reach
34. mush
35. church
36. march, marsh
37. clash
38. torch
39. porch
40. fish

Exercise 4

1. charmer
2. stylish
3. shorten
4. shameful
5. starchy
6. charter
7. shiver
8. cherish

9. brunch
10. ushers

Exercise 5

1. stylish
2. ushers
3. shameful
4. shiver
5. charmer
6. starchy
7. shorten
8. charter
9. brunch
10. cherish

Exercise 6

1. chair/man
2. ship/yard
3. shell/fish
4. stop/watch
5. sun/shine
6. match/maker
7. watch/man
8. shut/out
9. stop/watch
10. chalk/board
11. cheer/leader
12. sheep/skin
13. shoe/string
14. short/hand
15. sea/shell
16. touch/down
17. hitch/hike
18. latch/key
19. chamber/maid
20. shut/down

LESSON | 8

In this lesson, you'll learn about two more consonant pairs—*th* and *wh.* You'll also get more practice with substitution, which will help you increase the pool of words you can spell correctly.

THE PAIRING CONTINUES . . .

EXERCISE 1: EYEBALLING SPELLING LIST 8

Directions: Sweep your eyes across the line from left to right and back again. Do it quickly. Circle the word in each line that looks different from the others on that line.

Are you ready? Get set . . . Go!

1. whisper	whisper	whisker	whisper
2. whimper	whisper	whimper	whimper
3. ether	either	either	either
4. thirty	thirty	thirsty	thirty
5. white	white	while	white
6. smooth	sooth	smooth	smooth
7. thankful	thankful	tankful	thankful

8. wheel	wheel	while	wheel
9. whistle	whittle	whistle	whistle
10. whenever	whatever	whatever	whatever

Check your answers with the answer key at the end of this lesson.
My score for Exercise 1 is _____ out of 10.

 ## REFLECTION

In Lesson 7, you learned that the letters *ch* and *sh* are consonant pairs. In this lesson, there are two more consonant pairs. Go back to the words that are the same on each line in Exercise 1 and see if you can find these two pairs. Write them on the line. _____

If you said the consonant pairs are the letters *wh* and *th,* you're absolutely correct. Return to the list and circle the consonant pairs.

Move on to Exercise 2, Sound Inventory, to hear the sound of the consonant pairs.

 # EXERCISE 2: SOUND INVENTORY

Directions: Listen to yourself as you read each group of words aloud. **You must read the words out loud.** The letters and sounds in each group have something in common. Put a circle around the letters that are the same and then write that consonant pair on the line provided.

GROUP 1		**GROUP 2**	
why	wheat	thin	path
whale	when	thank	teeth
whip	white	then	wither
_____		_____	

In Group 1, the common letters are *wh.* Can you hear the sound of the letters *wh?* If you need help, use slash marks to break the words into sounds. The word *why* should be written as /wh/i/ (reminder: the letter *y* has an /i/ sound). The word *white* should be written as /wh/i/t/. Now can you hear the sound? It has the same sound as the letter *w* on the Letter/Sound Relationship Key and as found in the clue word **whisper.**

In Group 2, the common letters are *th.* Can you hear the sound of *th?* If you need help, use slash marks to break the words into sounds. The word *thin* should be written as /th/i/n/ and the word *then* should be written as /th/e/n/. Now can you hear the sound? It has the same sound as found in the clue words *the thinker*.

th Sounds

There is a slight difference between the /th/ sound in the word *the* and the /th/ sound in the word *thinker*. Say the word *the* aloud and pay careful attention to the vibrating sound of your lips. Say the word *thinker* aloud and pay attention to how different the /th/ sound is from the /th/ in the word *the*. There is a slight difference in sound, but all you need to remember is that both sounds are represented by the letters *th*.

It's a good idea to go through all the words in Group 1 and Group 2 and break them into sounds using slash marks. There are many words there to help you review the sounds you've learned in Lessons 1–7.

REFLECTION

The consonant pairs in this lesson are represented by the letters *wh* and *th*. How will the clue words help you? _____

Why is it important to remember the letters of each consonant pair?

_____

_____

Keep Practicing!

As you already know, clue words help you remember sounds. It's important to remember consonant pairs because they aren't as easy to hear as consonant blends. The next exercise will help you to reinforce the skills you learned in Lessons 1–8. Always remember this: **Spelling is the relationship between letters and sounds**. As you acquire more letter/sound relationships, you'll gain more skills to help you spell words correctly. The best way to learn is to *practice, practice, practice*.

EXERCISE 3: PRACTICE WITH SUBSTITUTION

Directions: Change the **first** consonant or the blend (two consonants) to one of the two consonant pairs you learned in this lesson. Use the clue words *whisper* and *thinker* to help you remember the letter/sound pair. Write the new word next to the original word on the provided line. The first three are done for you.

1. risk _____whisk_____   9. rank _____
2. pile _____while_____   10. dump _____
3. wink _____think_____   11. left _____
4. slip _____   12. bird _____
5. first _____   13. girl _____
6. corn _____   14. biter _____
7. dirty _____   15. feel _____
8. sick _____

Check your answers with the answer key at the end of this lesson.

Directions: This time, make changes to the consonant at the **end** of the word using the pairs *sh, ch,* and *th.* Write the new word on the provided line. The first one is done for you. In this exercise, use the endings *sh, ch,* and *th.* Note that some words can take more than one of these endings.

1. boom _____   9. teen _____
2. win _____   10. mob _____
3. mark _____   11. bread _____
4. rug _____   12. pan _____
5. churn _____   13. perk _____
6. bag _____   14. tool _____
7. bird _____   15. norm _____
8. scorn _____

Check your answers with the answer key at the end of this lesson.

My score for Exercise 3 is _____ out of 30.

EXERCISE 4: PRACTICE WRITING SPELLING LIST 8

Directions: Go back to Exercise 1. Look at the three words that are the same on each line. Write each of these words only once on the lines below. This would be a good time to have your study buddy dictate the words to you.

1. _____   6. _____
2. _____   7. _____
3. _____   8. _____
4. _____   9. _____
5. _____   10. _____

Consult your dictionary if the meaning of a word is unfamiliar to you.

Check your answers with the answer key at the end of this lesson.

My score for Exercise 4 is _____ out of 10.

EXERCISE 5: PRACTICE WRITING SPELLING LIST 8 IN CONTEXT

Directions: Use any word from Exercise 4 to complete each phrase. For added practice, rewrite the entire phrase in your own sentence on the provided line.

1. _____ for the gifts

   _____

2. a soft _____ in my ear

   _____

3. _____ or, neither nor

   _____

4. a high-pitched _____

   _____

5. _____ for a cold drink

   _____

6. either black or _____

   _____

7. _____ you want

   _____

8. invention of the _____

   _____

9. _____ as silk

   _____

10. a soft _____

    _____

Check your answers with the answer key at the end of this lesson. Only the words that go in the blanks are given, since everyone will create different sentences.

My score for Exercise 5 is _____ out of 10.

VARIATIONS

In some words, the letters *wh* produce another sound, as found in the beginning of the word *he*. Read the following words and listen for the first sound. Practice writing these words in your notebook.

who	whole	wholesome
wholesale	whose	whom

Challenge

Do you want more challenging words that use the /wh/ and /th/ sounds? Try these! Call on your study buddy to dictate them to you as you write them in your notebook. Consult your dictionary if you are unsure of the meanings of any of these words.

thermometer	thermostat	apathy	Sabbath
therapy	athletes	theatrical	thirteenth
whirlpool	whitewash	overwhelm	whimsical

EXERCISE 6: WHAT HAVE YOU LEARNED?

Directions: Circle all the consonant pairs (*ch, sh, th,* and *wh*) in these compound words. Then separate each word by writing the two words that make the compound word. The first one is done for you.

1. mushroom   _mush_   _room_
2. whirlwind   _____   _____
3. toothpaste   _____   _____
4. somewhere   _____   _____
5. witchcraft   _____   _____
6. toothache   _____   _____
7. wholesale   _____   _____
8. stagecoach   _____   _____
9. wishbone   _____   _____
10. whatever   _____   _____

Directions: Read each of the following sentences and write the word that has a consonant pair. This would be a good time for your study buddy to dictate the sentences to you as you write them in your notebook.

11. Be thankful for whatever you have.
12. Thanksgiving is the fourth Thursday in November.
13. The peppermint toothpaste is on the third shelf.
14. Cheers will be heard around the world for the thousands of Olympic athletes.
15. The chapters in his childhood revealed much pain.
16. Turn the wheel thirty times.
17. Why whisper such good news?

18. The stagecoach will drive north to Whisper County.
19. What is the path of the thunderstorm?
20. Either use the chopsticks or ask for a fork.

Check your answers with the answer key at the end of this lesson.

My score for Exercise 6 is _____ out of 20.

ANSWER KEY FOR LESSON 8
Exercise 1
1. whisker
2. whisper
3. ether
4. thirsty
5. while
6. sooth
7. tankful
8. while
9. whittle
10. whenever

Exercise 3
1. whisk
2. while
3. think
4. whip
5. thirst
6. thorn
7. thirty
8. thick
9. thank
10. thump
11. theft
12. third
13. whirl
14. whiter
15. wheel
16. booth
17. wish, with

18. marsh, march
19. rush
20. church
21. bath, bash
22. birth, birch
23. scorch
24. teeth
25. moth
26. breath
27. path
28. perch
29. tooth
30. north

Exercise 4
1. whisper
2. whimper
3. either
4. thirty
5. white
6. smooth
7. thankful
8. wheel
9. whistle
10. whatever

Exercise 5
1. thankful
2. whisper
3. either
4. whistle
5. thirsty
6. white
7. whatever
8. wheel
9. smooth
10. whimper

Exercise 6
1. mush   room
2. whirl   wind
3. tooth   paste
4. some   where
5. witch   craft
6. tooth   ache

7. whole   sale
8. stage   coach
9. wish   bone
10. what   ever
11. thankful, whatever
12. Thanksgiving, fourth, Thursday
13. the, toothpaste, third, shelf
14. cheers, the, thousands, athletes
15. the, chapters, childhood, much
16. the, wheel, thirty
17. why, whisper, such
18. the, stagecoach, north, Whisper
19. what, path, the, thunderstorm
20. either, the, chopsticks

LESSON | 9

In this lesson you will learn the last three **consonant pairs**. Believe it or not, you've already covered more than half of the letter/sound relationships! Get ready to spell more challenging words.

THE FINAL PAIRS

EXERCISE 1: EYEBALLING SPELLING LIST 9

Directions: Sweep your eyes across the line from left to right and back again. Do it quickly. Circle the word in each line that looks different from the others on that line.

Are you ready? Get set . . . Go!

1. pheasant	pheasant	pleasant	pheasant
2. graphing	grasping	graphing	graphing
3. spears	spheres	spheres	spheres
4. phrase	phrase	phrase	phase
5. photograph	photograph	phonograph	photograph
6. gangplank	gangplank	gangplank	gangway
7. bankrupt	banking	bankrupt	bankrupt

8.	swinging	swinging	swinging	stinging
9.	roughness	roughneck	roughneck	roughneck
10.	toughen	toughen	toughen	touring

Check your answers with the answer key at the end of this lesson.
My score for Exercise 1 is _____ out of 10.

REFLECTION

In Lessons 7 and 8, you learned that the letters *ch, sh, wh,* and *th* are consonant pairs. Go back to the words that are the same on each line in Exercise 1. There are three more consonant pairs. See if you can find them and write them on the following line. _____
_____

If you located the letters *gh, ph,* and *ng* as three more consonant pairs, you're getting very good at this. Return to the list and circle the consonant pairs, then move on to Exercise 2, Sound Inventory, to hear what they sound like.

EXERCISE 2: SOUND INVENTORY

Directions: Listen to yourself as you read each group of words aloud. **You must read the words out loud.** The letters and sounds in each group have something in common. Put a circle around the letters that are the same in each group and write them on the lines provided.

GROUP 1		GROUP 2	
sphere	rough	bang	thanking
phone	cough	thing	swinging
graph	tough	gong	singing

____ ____   ____

In Group 1, the common letters are *ph* and *gh*. Can you hear the sound of the letters *ph* and *gh*? If you need help, use slash marks to break the words into sounds. The sound in Group 1 is represented by the letter *f*, so the word *photo* should be written /f/o/t/o/, and the word *rough* should be written as /r/u/f/. Now can you hear the sound? It has the same sound as the letter *f* on the Letter/Sound Relationship Key and as found in the clue phrase *rough graph.*

In Group 2, the common letters are *ng*. Can you hear the sound of the letters *ng?* To help you isolate the sound, say the word *sing* aloud. Then take away the letter *s* and say *ing*. It's easier to say the sound *ng* when a vowel precedes it. Say the following *ng* examples aloud and notice that each is preceded by a short vowel sound: *ing, ang, ung, eng, ong*. It may help you to break the words into sounds. For example, the word *thing* looks like /th/i/ng/. Now can you hear the sound? It has the same sound as found in the clue word *swing*.

The consonant pair *ng,* represented by the letters /ng/, can appear in the **middle** or the **end** of the word. You will never write it as a beginning sound in the English language. As you saw in Group 1, the /f/ sound, represented by the letters *gh*, usually appears at the **end** of a word. When the letters *gh* appear at the beginning of a word, as found in the word *ghost,* they make a different sound, in this case simply the sound /g/, where the *h* is silent. The sound /f/, represented by the letters *ph*, can be found anywhere in a word.

REFLECTION

The consonant pairs in this lesson are represented by the letters *ph, gh,* and *ng*. What two consonant pairs make the same sound? _____
Which consonant pair will never appear in the beginning of a word?

_____

How can clue words help you? _____

_____

The consonant pairs represented by the letters *ph* and *gh* have the same sound (except when *gh* appears at the beginning of a word and makes something other than the /f/ sound). The consonant pair represented by the letters *ng* will never appear at the beginning of a word. As you probably know by now, letters represent many sounds. In the English language, the 26-letter alphabet represents over 40 sounds. Believe it or not, you've already studied more than half of them!

Continue your study by moving on to Exercise 3, which will reinforce the letter/sound relationships that you have learned in this lesson.

EXERCISE 3: PRACTICE WITH SUBSTITUTION

Directions: Change the first consonant or the **blend** (two consonants) to the letters that represent the sound you hear in the clue word *graph.*

1. vase _____
2. bone _____
3. pony _____
4. tonics _____
5. pleasant _____

Directions: Change the **ending** consonant pair to the letters that represent the sound you hear in the clue word *swing*.

6. rich _____
7. rash _____
8. path _____
9. bath _____
10. such _____

Check your answers with the answer key at the end of this lesson.

My score for Exercise 3 is _____ out of 10.

EXERCISE 4: PRACTICE WRITING SPELLING LIST 9

Directions: Go back to Exercise 1. Look at the three words that are the same on each line. Write each of these words only once on the lines below. This would be a good time to have your study buddy dictate the words to you.

1. _____   6. _____
2. _____   7. _____
3. _____   8. _____
4. _____   9. _____
5. _____   10. _____

Consult your dictionary if the meaning of a word is unfamiliar to you.

Check your answers with the answer key at the end of this lesson.

My score for Exercise 4 is _____ out of 10.

EXERCISE 5: PRACTICE WRITING SPELLING LIST 9 IN CONTEXT

Directions: Use any word from Exercise 4 to complete each phrase. For added practice, rewrite the entire phrase in your own sentence on the provided line.

1. a _____ resting in its nest

   _____

2. _____ the rules

   _____

3. _____ the data

   _____

4. a wooden _____ on the ship

   _____

5. roll the _____

   _____

6. a three-word _____

   _____

7. pose for the _____

   _____

8. _____ back and forth

   _____

9. a _____ hangout

   _____

10. a _____ business

    _____

Check your answers with the answer key at the end of this lesson. Only the words that go in the blanks are given, since everyone will create different sentences.

My score for Exercise 5 is _____ out of 10.

VARIATIONS

In only a few words, the letters *gh* at the beginning of a word sound like /g/, as in *goat*. Most of these words are related; they have to do with ghosts. Practice writing these words in your notebook.

ghostly	**gh**ostwriter
ghastly	**gh**oulish

Do you want more challenging words that use the /f/ sound? Try these! Call on your study buddy to dictate them to you as you write them in your notebook. Consult your dictionary if you're unsure of any of the meanings of these words.

peripheral   pam**ph**let   hemis**ph**ere   trium**ph**ant

phosphorus   **ph**antom   cello**ph**ane   **ph**ysical

graphic   gra**ph**ite

EXERCISE 6: WHAT HAVE YOU LEARNED?

Directions: Circle all the consonant pairs *(ph, gh, ng)* in the following compound words; then separate each word by writing the two words that make them up. The first one is done for you.

1. fingerpaint   *finger*   *paint*
2. fingernail   _____   _____
3. singsong   _____   _____
4. singlehanded   _____   _____
5. roughneck   _____   _____
6. speakerphone   _____   _____
7. ringleader   _____   _____
8. ringworm   _____   _____
9. ringmaster   _____   _____
10. fingerprint   _____   _____

Directions: Read each of the following sentences and write the words that have a consonant pair you have learned. This would be a good time for your study buddy to dictate the sentences to you as you write them in your notebook.

11. The Philadelphia Philharmonic will perform on the first Thursday in March.
12. Unknowingly, the pheasants posed for the photographer.
13. Three gongs mean to leave right away.
14. Bang on the door three times and I will let you in.
15. The Earth is shaped like a sphere.
16. Can you phrase that one more time?
17. Draw the lines on the graph with a red pen.
18. The pendulum swings back and forth.
19. Ring the phone three times and then hang up.
20. Tell us the truth about the phantom.

Check your answers with the answer key at the end of this lesson.

My score for Exercise 6 is _____ out of 20.

ANSWER KEY FOR LESSON 9

Exercise 1

1. pleasant
2. grasping
3. spears
4. phase
5. phonograph
6. gangway
7. banking
8. stinging
9. roughness
10. touring

Exercise 3

1. phase
2. phone
3. phony
4. phonics
5. pheasant
6. ring
7. rang
8. pang
9. bang
10. sung

Exercise 4

1. pheasant
2. graphing
3. spheres
4. phrase
5. photograph
6. gangplank
7. bankrupt
8. swinging
9. roughneck
10. toughen

Exercise 5

1. pheasant
2. toughen
3. graphing
4. gangplank
5. sphere
6. phrase
7. photograph
8. swinging
9. roughneck
10. bankrupt

Exercise 6

1. finger   paint
2. finger   nail
3. sing   song
4. single   handed
5. rough   neck
6. speaker   phone
7. ring   leader
8. ring   worm
9. ring   master
10. finger   print
11. the, Philadelphia, Philhar-monic, Thursday, March
12. unknowingly, the, pheasants, photographer
13. three, gongs (There is no mistake; the word *right* does not belong here. See Lesson 3.)
14. bang, the, three
15. the, Earth, shaped, sphere
16. phrase, that
17. the, graph, with
18. the, swings, forth
19. ring, the, phone, three, then, hang
20. truth, the, phantom

LESSON | 10

So far, you have learned that each consonant has only one sound. However, in this lesson you'll see that some consonants have two sounds. To differentiate between the two sounds, one will be called **hard** and the other will be called **soft**.

THE SOFTENING OF CONSONANTS

EXERCISE 1: EYEBALLING SPELLING LIST 10

Directions: Sweep your eyes across the line from left to right and back again. Do it quickly. Circle the word in each line that looks different from the others on that line.

Are you ready? Get set . . . Go!

1. celebrate	celebrate	celibate	celebrate
2. decent	decent	descent	decent
3. palace	place	palace	palace
4. centerpiece	centerpiece	centerpiece	certainty
5. invoice	invoice	device	invoice
6. refrigerator	regenerator	refrigerator	refrigerator
7. average	average	acreage	average
8. germs	gems	gems	gems

87

| 9. pager | pages | pager | pager |
| 10. agents | agents | angels | agents |

Check your answers with the answer key at the end of this lesson.
My score for Exercise 1 is _____ out of 10.

REFLECTION

Go back to the words that are the same on each line in Exercise 1. Locate the letters *c* and *g*. What kind of letter follows the letters *c* and *g*?

_____

You should have seen that a vowel always follows the letters *c* and *g* in the words above. Vowels are the only clue for understanding the concept of two sounds for one consonant. Move on to Exercise 2, Sound Inventory, to hear the sounds in this lesson.

EXERCISE 2: SOUND INVENTORY

Directions: Listen to yourself as you read each group of words aloud. **You must read the words out loud.** The letters and sounds in each group have something in common. Put a circle around the letters that are the same in each group and then write them on the lines provided.

GROUP 1
cell	voice
city	lacy
cent	recite

_____

GROUP 2
cake	music
cord	magic
cub	act

_____

GROUP 3
gems	agent
germs	angel
gist	cage

_____

GROUP 4
girl	ugly
grow	beg
grass	rug

_____

In Group 1, the common letter is *c*. Can you hear the sound of the letter *c*? If you need help, use slash marks to break the words into sounds. The sound in Group 1 is the same as the letter *s*, so the word *city* should be written /s/i/t/e/. This sound is called the **soft** sound of the letter *c*. It has the same sound as the letter *s* on the Letter/Sound Relationship Key and as the letter *c* in the clue word *celery*.

In Group 2, the common letter is also *c*. Can you hear the sound of this letter *c?* If you need help, use slash marks to break the words into sounds using the letter/sound strategy. The sound in Group 2 is the same as the letter *k,* so the word *cake* should be written /k/a/k/. This sound is called the **hard** sound of the letter *c*. It has the same sound as the letter *k* on the Letter/Sound Relationship Key and as found in the clue word *cake*.

In Group 3, the common letter is *g*. Can you hear the sound of the letter *g?* If you need help, use slash marks to break the words into sounds using the letter/sound strategy. The sound in Group 3 is the same as the letter *j,* so the word *gems* should be written /j/e/m/s/. This sound is called the **soft** sound of the letter *g*. It has the same sound as the letter *j* on the Letter/Sound Relationship Key and as found in the clue word *George*.

In Group 4, the common letter is also *g*. Can you hear the sound of this letter *g?* If you need help, use slash marks to break the words into sounds. The sound in Group 4 is the same as the letter *g,* so the word *gate* should be written /g/a/t/. This sound is called the **hard** sound of the letter *g*. It has the same sound as the letter *g* on the Letter/Sound Relationship Key and as found in the clue word *goat*.

 ## REFLECTION

What consonants did you learn about in this lesson? _____

What can you say about the sounds of the consonants?

_____

_____

What will help you decide whether a sound is soft or hard?

_____

The consonants in this lesson are the letters *c* and *g*. The letter *c* has a soft and hard sound, and the letter *g* has a soft and hard sound. The following is a general rule:

> **If either *e* or *i* follows the consonant *c* or *g*, the sound**
> **is *usually* (but not always) soft.**

For practice with the soft consonants, move on to Exercise 3.

EXERCISE 3: PRACTICE WITH SUBSTITUTION

Directions: Change the first consonant to the sound of soft *c*.

1. dent _____
2. pity _____
3. bell _____
4. renter _____
5. lease _____

Directions: Change the first consonant to the soft sound of *g*.

6. venerate _____
7. term _____
8. list _____
9. lender _____
10. terminate _____

Check your answers with the answer key at the end of this lesson.

My score for Exercise 3 is _____ out of 10.

EXERCISE 4: PRACTICE WRITING SPELLING LIST 10

Directions: Go back to Exercise 1. Look at the three words that are the same on each line. Write each of these words only once on the lines below. This would be a good time to have your study buddy dictate the words to you.

1. _____
2. _____
3. _____
4. _____
5. _____

6. _____
7. _____
8. _____
9. _____
10. _____

Consult your dictionary if the meaning of a word is unfamiliar to you.

Check your answers with the answer key at the end of this lesson.

My score for Exercise 4 is _____ out of 10.

EXERCISE 5: PRACTICE WRITING SPELLING LIST 10 IN CONTEXT

Directions: Use any word from Exercise 4 to complete each phrase. For added practice, rewrite the entire phrase in your own sentence on the provided line.

1. insurance _____

   _____

2. a digital _____

   _____

3. _____ a holiday

   _____

4. mailing the _____

   _____

5. a _____, hardworking person

   _____

6. shiny _____ in a necklace

   _____

7. the _____ score

   _____

8. milk in the _____

   _____

9. a flowering _____

   _____

10. a king's _____

    _____

Check your answers with the answer key at the end of this lesson. Only the words that go in the blanks are given, since everyone will create different sentences.

My score for Exercise 5 is _____ out of 10.

VARIATIONS

In some words, the letters *ge* are preceded by the letter *d*, as in the word *judge*. In such words, the consonant letter *g* is a soft sound and the letter *d* is silent. Circle the letters *dge* in each word. Practice writing them or have your study buddy dictate them to you.

judge	fudge	budge	ridge
bridge	wedge	hedge	pledge
ledge	badge	edge	lodge
sludge	smudge	grudge	

A few common words, including *girl*, *get*, and *gimmick*, have a hard /g/ sound even though they have *e* or *i* after the *g*.

Do you want more challenging words that use the /c/ and /g/ sounds? Try these! Call on your study buddy to dictate them to you as you write them in your notebook. Consult your dictionary if you need to so that you can use the words correctly.

cylinder	ceiling	innocent	cellular
cement	December	decimate	voiceless
process	recess	spicy	cemetery

tragedy	general	genocide	generate
Germany	generosity	plunger	revenge
gelatin	germicidal	refrigerator	

EXERCISE 6: WHAT HAVE YOU LEARNED?

Directions: Use words from Exercise 4 to complete the following sentences.

1. Which word means a bill to be paid? _____

2. Which word means a person who is a representative?

   _____

3. Which word means a decoration for the center of a table?

   _____

4. Which word means precious stones? _____

5. Which words means proper, appropriate, or kind?

   _____

Directions: Complete each sentence by choosing one word.

6. When will you _____ your next birthday? (celebrate, celibate)

7. The agent's _____ rang endlessly. (cellophane, cell phone)

8. The gypsy performed _____ and the man was healed. (manic, magic)

LEARNINGEXPRESS

LEARNINGEXPRESS

20 Academy Street, P.O. Box 7100, Norwalk, CT 06852-9879

~FREE!~ TEN TIPS TO PASSING ANY TEST

To provide you with the test prep and career information you need, we would appreciate your help. Please answer the following questions and return this postage paid survey. As our Thank You, we will send you our "Ten Tips To Passing Any Test" – surefire ways to score your best on classroom and/or job-related exams.

Name : _____

Address : _____

_____

Age : _____   Sex : ☐ Male   ☐ Female

Highest Level of School Completed : ☐ High School ☐ College

1) I am currently ;

    A student — Year/level: _____

    Employed — Job title: _____

    Other — Please explain: _____

2) Jobs/careers of interest to me are :

    1. _____

    2. _____

    3. _____

3) If you are a student, did your guidance/career counselor provide you with job information/materials? _____

    Name & Location of School: _____

_____

_____

_____

4) What newspapers and/or magazines do you subscribe to or read regularly? _____

_____

5) Do you own a computer? _____

    Do you have Internet access? _____

    How often do you go on-line? _____

6) Have you purchased career-related materials from bookstores?

_____

    If yes, list recent examples: _____

_____

7) Which radio stations do you listen to regularly (please give call letters and city name)?

_____

_____

8) How did you hear about this LearningExpress book?

    An ad? _____

    If so, where? _____

    An order form in the back of another book? _____

    A recommendation? _____

    A bookstore? _____

    Other? _____

9) Title of the book this card came from:

_____

LearningExpress books are also available in the test prep/study guide section of your local bookstore.

LearningExpress

The new leader in test preparation and career guidance!

LearningExpress is an affiliate of Random House, Inc.

9. The Queen of England resides at Buckingham
   _____. (Palace, Place)
10. The _____ meeting will be held in the center hall.
    (lodge, ledge)

Directions: Circle all the words in the following sentences that have a soft *c* and *g*.

11. Add cinnamon spice to the hot apple cider.
12. Cement is a process developed by the ancient Romans.
13. The ceilings in the palace were painted with gold leaf.
14. The death of the general is truly a tragedy.
15. Gelatin is easy to digest.
16. It is too cold for the seeds to germinate in December.
17. That baby has such an angelic face.
18. It is too cool in the cellar to store the spices there.
19. The police officer's badge was removed by the judge.
20. Recite the pledge of allegiance.

Directions: Separate the words you circled in sentences 11–20 by putting all the soft *c* words in one column and all the soft *g* words in the other column.

Words with Soft *c*	**Words with Soft *g***

Check your answers with the answer key at the end of this lesson.
My score for Exercise 6 is _____ out of 20.

ANSWER KEY FOR LESSON 10

Exercise 1
1. celibate
2. descent
3. place
4. certainty
5. device
6. regenerator
7. acreage
8. germs
9. pages
10. angels

Exercise 3
1. cent
2. city
3. cell
4. center
5. cease
6. generate
7. germ
8. gist
9. gender
10. germinate

Exercise 4
1. celebrate
2. decent
3. palace
4. centerpiece
5. invoice
6. refrigerator
7. average
8. gems
9. pager
10. agents

Exercise 5
1. agents
2. pager
3. celebrate
4. invoice
5. decent
6. gems
7. average
8. refrigerator
9. centerpiece
10. palace

Exercise 6
1. invoice
2. agent
3. centerpiece
4. gems
5. decent
6. celebrate
7. cell phone
8 magic
9. Palace
10. lodge
11. cinnamon, spice, cider
12. cement, process
13. ceilings, palace
14. general, tragedy
15. gelatin, digest
16. germinate, December
17. angelic, face
18. cellar, spices
19. police, officer's, badge, judge
20. recite, pledge, allegiance

Words with Soft c

cinnamon
spice
cider
cement
process
ceilings
Palace
December
face
cellar
spices
police
recite
officer's

Words with Soft g

general
tragedy
gelatin
digest
germinate
angelic
badge
judge
pledge
allegiance

LESSON | 11

The consonants in this lesson have unusual letter/sound relationships. That's why we call them the "oddball consonants." When you finish this lesson, you will be familiar with the special spelling strategies involving the letters *x* and *q*.

THE ODDBALL CONSONANTS

EXERCISE 1: EYEBALLING SPELLING LIST 11

Directions: Sweep your eyes across the line from left to right and back again. Do it quickly. Circle the word in each line that looks different from the others on that line.

Are you ready? Get set . . . Go!

1. quit	quit	quit	quilt
2. squirt	squirt	squint	squirt
3. quality	qualify	qualify	qualify
4. quarry	quarry	quaggy	quarry
5. sequels	sequels	sequins	sequels
6. sixty	sticky	sixty	sixty
7. exist	exit	exit	exit

8. exact	exact	exult	exact
9. explore	explore	explore	expose
10. extract	extract	exact	extract

Check your answers with the answer key at the end of this lesson.
My score for Exercise 1 is _____ out of 10.

REFLECTION

Go back to the words that are the same on each line in Exercise 1. Locate the letters *x* and *q*. Each of these letters has a partner.

What letter is the partner of the letter *x*? _____

What letter is the partner of the letter *q*? _____

The letter *x* usually has the letter *e* or another vowel as a partner, and the letter *q* always has the letter *u* as a partner. The unusual thing about these letters is their sound. Move on to Exercise 2, Sound Inventory, to hear the sounds of these oddball consonants.

EXERCISE 2: SOUND INVENTORY

Directions: Listen to yourself as you read each group of words aloud. **You must read the words out loud.** The letters and sounds in each group have something in common. Put a circle around the letters that are the same in each group and then write them on the lines provided.

GROUP 1	GROUP 2	GROUP 3
quit	exit	box
queen	explode	six
quick	exist	fox
quack	extend	tax
_____	_____	_____

In Group 1, the common letters are *qu.* Can you hear the sound of the letters *qu*? If you need help, use slash marks to break the words into sounds. The word *quit* should be written as /k/w/i/t/ and the word *queen* should be written as k/w/e/n/. Now can you hear the sound? The letters *qu* represent the combined sound of /k/ and /w/, as found in the clue word **quilt.**

In Group 2, the common letters are *ex.* Can you hear the sound of the letters *ex?* If you need help, use slash marks to break the words into sounds. The word *exit* should be written as /e/k/s/i/t/ and the word *extend* should be written as /e/k/s/t/e/n/d/. Now can you hear the sound? The letters *ex* represent the sound of the combination /e/k/s/, as found in the clue word **ex**tract.

In Group 3, the common letter is *x*. Can you hear the sound of the letter *x?* If you need help, use slash marks to break the words into sounds. The word *box* should be written as /b/o/k/s/ and the word *tax* should be written as /t/a/k/s/. Now can you hear the sound? The letter *x* represents the sound of the two consonants /k/s/ as found in the clue word **ex**tract.

REFLECTION

What consonants did you learn about in this lesson? _____

What sounds do these consonants represent? _____

Why are these consonants called the oddball consonants? _____

_____

The consonants in this lesson are represented by the letters *qu* and *x*. The letters *qu* represent the sound of /k/w/ and the letter *x* represents the sound of /k/s/. If the letter *e* precedes the letter *x*, you hear a syllable that sounds like /e/k/s/.

These consonants are called the oddball consonants because they have strange letter/sound relationships. The letter *x*, a single consonant, makes two sounds: /k/s/. The consonant letter *q* is **always** followed by the letter *u* and together they make the sound /k/w/. For practice with these consonants, move on to Exercise 3.

EXERCISE 3: PRACTICE WITH SUBSTITUTION

Directions: Change the first consonant in each word to the vowel/consonant combination you hear in the beginning of the word *extract*. The first one is done for you.

1. sit   _____*exit*_____

2. pact   _____

3. mile   _____

4. fist   _____

5. fit   _____

Directions: Change the first consonant in each word to the consonant/vowel combination you hear in the beginning of the word *quilt.* The first one is done for you.

6. bit   _____*quit*_____

7. rail   _____

8. teen   _____

9. paint   _____

10. river   _____

Directions: Change the first consonant in each word to the consonant/vowel combination you hear in the word *squirt*. The first one is done for you.

11. leaky   _____*squeaky*_____

12. dirt   _____

13. hint   _____

14. freeze   _____

15. deal   _____

Directions: Change the final consonant to the letter *x*.

16. sin   _____*six*_____

17. wag   _____

18. fog   _____

19. tap   _____

20. fat   _____

Check your answers with the answer key at the end of this lesson.

My score for Exercise 3 is _____ out of 20.

EXERCISE 4: PRACTICE WRITING SPELLING LIST 11

Directions: Go back to Exercise 1. Look at the three words that are the same on each line. Write each of these words only once on the lines below. This would be a good time to have your study buddy dictate the words to you.

1. _____   **6.** _____

2. _____   **7.** _____

3. _____   **8.** _____

4. _____   **9.** _____

5. _____   **10.** _____

Consult your dictionary if the meaning of a word is unfamiliar to you.

Check your answers with the answer key at the end of this lesson.

My score for Exercise 4 is _____ out of 10.

EXERCISE 5: PRACTICE WRITING SPELLING LIST 11 IN CONTEXT

Directions: Use any word from Exercise 4 to complete each phrase. For added practice, rewrite the entire phrase in your own sentence on the provided line.

1. lemon _____ for flavoring

_____

2. _____ a job

_____

3. _____ water

_____

4. _____ the unknown

_____

5. _____ for the position

_____

6. add the _____ amount

_____

7. a stone _____

_____

8. go out the _____

_____

9. two _____ to the movie

_____

10. _____ years old

_____

Check your answers with the answer key at the end of this lesson. Only the words that go in the blanks are given, since everyone will create different sentences.

My score for Exercise 5 is _____ out of 10.

Do you want more challenging words that contain the letters *x* and *qu?* Try these! Call on your study buddy to dictate them to you as you write them in your notebook. Consult your dictionary if necessary so that you can use the words correctly.

exonerate	exhibit	expensive	experiment
except	exhale	expound	exploit
external	expect	exceed	exchange
existence	extraction	exercise	oxide
fixate	sixteenth	oxygen	

quicksand	sequence	aquatic	quintet
quiet	quite		

EXERCISE 6: WHAT HAVE YOU LEARNED?

In Lesson 10, you learned about the softening of the consonants *c* and *g.* In this lesson, you learned about the oddball consonants *x* and *qu.* The next exercise reviews all of these spelling skills.

Directions: Read each compound word **aloud.** Rewrite each compound word as two words on the lines provided.

1. gentleman _____ _____
2. expressway _____ _____
3. taxpayer _____ _____
4. bridgework _____ _____
5. facelift _____ _____
6. pacemaker _____ _____
7. policeman _____ _____
8. guardrail _____ _____
9. headquarters _____ _____
10. earthquake _____ _____

Directions: Read each sentence **aloud** and circle the words that have softening consonants or oddball consonants. This would be a great time to have your study buddy dictate the sentences to you.

11. Cross the bridge to the queen's palace.
12. Squeeze lemon extract through the cake mix.
13. Your voice is unclear on that cell phone.

14. Recite the magic words and the gypsy will appear.
15. Connect the cables to the microprocessor.
16. Quench your thirst at the refreshment center.
17. Does your fax machine have a digital quartz display?
18. Export the quartz stones from the quarry to Germany.
19. Meet the general at the army headquarters.
20. Cover the angel hair pasta with cellophane.

My score for Exercise 6 is _____ out of 20.

ANSWER KEY FOR LESSON 11

Exercise 1
1. quilt
2. squint
3. quality
4. quaggy
5. sequins
6. sticky
7. exist
8. exult
9. expose
10. exact

13. squint
14. squeeze
15. squeal
16. six
17. wax
18. fox
19. tax
20. fax

Exercise 3
1. exit
2. exact
3. exile
4. exist
5. exit
6. quit
7. quail
8. queen
9. quaint
10. quiver
11. squeaky
12. squirt

Exercise 4
1. quit
2. squirt
3. qualify
4. quarry
5. sequels
6. sixty
7. exit
8. exact
9. explore
10. extract

Exercise 5

1. extract
2. quit
3. squirt
4. explore
5. qualify
6. exact
7. quarry
8. exit
9. sequels
10. sixty

Exercise 6

1. gentle   man
2. express   way
3. tax   payer
4. bridge   work
5. face   lift

6. pace   maker
7. police   man
8. guard   rail
9. head   quarters
10. earth   quake
11. bridge, queen's, palace
12. Squeeze, extract, mix
13. voice, cell
14. Recite, magic, gypsy
15. processor
16. Quench, center
17. fax, digital, quartz
18. Export, quartz, quarry, Germany
19. general, headquarters
20. angel, cellophane

LESSON | 12

SILENCE!

So far, the lessons in this book have taught spelling skills by emphasizing letter/sound relationships. This lesson, however, keys in on letters that make no sound. These are some of the most difficult letters to remember. Although they may be absolutely silent, you still have to write them if you want people to know what you mean.

EXERCISE 1: EYEBALLING SPELLING LIST 12

Directions: Sweep your eyes across the line from left to right and back again. Do it quickly. Circle the word in each line that looks different from the others on that line.

Are you ready? Get set . . . Go!

1. wreath	wreath	wreath	wrath
2. wrench	wrench	wreck	wrench
3. wrestling	whistling	wrestling	wrestling
4. rhymes	rhythms	rhythms	rhythms
5. rhinoceros	rhinoceros	rhombus	rhinoceros
6. rhinestone	rhinoceros	rhinestone	rhinestone
7. knowledge	knowledge	acknowledge	knowledge
8. kneads	knees	kneads	kneads

9. gnats	gnaws	gnaws	gnaws
10. resign	design	design	design

Check your answers with the answer key at the end of this lesson.
My score for Exercise 1 is _____ out of 10.

REFLECTION

Go back to the words that are the same on each line in Exercise 1. Locate the letters *wr*, *rh*, *kn*, and *gn*. These letters are partners. When they're together, only one is allowed to speak. In other words, only one out of the two letters represents a sound. How will you know which letter represents a sound? You can find out by doing Exercise 2, Sound Inventory.

EXERCISE 2: SOUND INVENTORY

Directions: Listen to yourself as you read each group of words aloud. **You must read the words out loud.** The letters and sounds in each group have something in common. Put a circle around the letters that are the same in each group and then write them on the lines provided.

GROUP 1
wrap
wreath
wren

_____

GROUP 2
rhyme
Rhine
rhumba

_____

GROUP 3
knit
know
knot

_____

GROUP 4
gnat   sign
gnaw   resign
gnarl   design

_____

In Group 1, the common letters are *wr*. Can you hear the sound of the letters *wr*? Which letter is silent? If you need help, use slash marks to break the words into sounds. The word *wrap* should be written as /r/a/p/, and the word *wreath* should be written as /r/e/th/. Now can you hear the sound? The letter *w* is silent and the letter *r* has the sound found in the clue word *radio*.

In Group 2, the common letters are *rh*. Can you hear the sound of the letters *rh*? Which letter is silent? If you need help, use slash marks to break the words into sounds. The word *rhyme* should be written as /r/i/m/ and the word *Rhine* should be written as /r/i/n/. Now can you hear the sound? The letter *h* is silent and the letter *r* has the sound found in the clue word *radio*.

In Group 3, the common letters are *kn*. Can you hear the sound of the letters *kn*? Which letter is silent? If you need help, use slash marks to break the words into sounds. The word *knot* should be written as /n/o/t/ and the word *knit* should be written as /n/i/t/. Now can you hear the sound? The letter *k* is silent and the letter *n* has the sound found in the clue word *needle*.

In Group 4, the common letters are *gn*. Can you hear the sound of the letters *gn*? Which letter is silent? If you need help, use slash marks to break the words into sounds. The word *gnat* should be written as /n/a/t/ and the word *sign* should be written /s/i/n/. Now can you hear the sound? The letter *g* is silent and the letter *n* has the sound found in the clue word *needle*.

REFLECTION

What consonants did you learn about in this lesson? _____

What sound do *kn* and *gn* represent? _____

What sound do *wr* and *rh* represent? _____

Where are these silent letters located in the words? _____

The sound of the letter *n*, as found in the clue word *needle*, is represented by the letters *kn* and *gn*. The sound of the letter *r*, as found in the clue word *radio*, is represented by the letters *wr* and *rh*. Most of the time, silent letters are located at the beginning of a word. The letters *gn*, though, can be located both at the beginning and at the end of a word. For practice with these silent letters, move on to Exercise 3.

EXERCISE 3: PRACTICE WITH SUBSTITUTION

Directions: Remove the first consonant and substitute it with the letters *kn, gn, wr,* or *rh.*

1. neck _____   **6.** list _____

2. rack _____   **7.** cob _____

3. bats _____   **8.** buckle _____

4. raw _____   **9.** low _____

5. line _____   **10.** lock _____

Check your answers with the answer key at the end of this lesson.

My score for Exercise 3 is _____ out of 10.

EXERCISE 4: PRACTICE WRITING SPELLING LIST 12

Directions: Go back to Exercise 1. Look at the three words that are the same on each line. Write each of these words only once on the lines below. This would be a good time to have your study buddy dictate the words to you.

1. _____   6. _____
2. _____   7. _____
3. _____   8. _____
4. _____   9. _____
5. _____   10. _____

Consult your dictionary if the meaning of a word is unfamiliar to you.

Check your answers with the answer key at the end of this lesson.

My score for Exercise 4 is _____ out of 10.

EXERCISE 5: PRACTICE WRITING SPELLING LIST 12 IN CONTEXT

Directions: Use the words from Exercise 4 to complete the phrases below. For added practice, rewrite the entire phrase in your own sentence on the line provided.

1. a gerbil _____

_____

2. _____ the dough

_____

3. hang the holiday _____

_____

4. a pipe _____

_____

5. a _____ match

_____

6. listen for the _____

_____

7. _____ a wedding dress

_____

8. a _____ necklace

_____

9. a book of _____

_____

10. the endangered _____

_____

Check your answers with the answer key at the end of this lesson. Only the words that go in the blanks are given, since everyone will create different sentences.

My score for Exercise 5 is _____ out of 10.

Challenge Do you want more challenging words with the combinations *kn, gn, wr,* and *rh?* Try these! Call on your study buddy to dictate them to you as you write them in your notebook. Consult your dictionary if you need to so that you can use the words correctly.

knuckle	knighthood	acknowledgment
wrapper	wrinkle	wristband
rheumatism	rhetorical	rhombus
benign	campaign	

EXERCISE 6: WHAT HAVE YOU LEARNED?

Directions: Read each compound word **aloud.** Then rewrite each compound word on the lines provided as two separate words.

1. wrongdoer _____ _____

2. wristband _____ _____

3. doorknob _____ _____

4. knockout _____ _____

5. knapsack _____ _____

6. shipwreck _____ _____

7. kneepads _____ _____

8. signpost _____ _____

9. signboard _____ _____

10. kneecap _____ _____

Directions: Read each phrase **aloud** and circle the words that have the silent letters you learned in this lesson.

11. a pinecone wreath
12. real estate signs on the lawn
13. the queen reigns
14. the foreign invaders
15. a gnarled tree
16. a knight in shining armor
17. a rhyming word
18. wrapping presents
19. design women's clothing
20. knit a sweater

Check your answers with the answer key at the end of this lesson.
My score for Exercise 6 is _____ out of 20.

ANSWER KEY FOR LESSON 12
Exercise 1
1. wrath
2. wreck
3. whistling
4. rhymes
5. rhombus
6. rhinoceros
7. acknowledge
8. knees
9. gnats
10. resign

9. know
10. knock

Exercise 4
1. wreath
2. wrench
3. wrestling
4. rhythms
5. rhinoceros
6. rhinestone
7. knowledge
8. kneads
9. gnaws
10. design

Exercise 3
1. wreck
2. knack
3. gnats
4. gnaw
5. Rhine
6. wrist
7. knob
8. knuckle

Exercise 5
1. gnaws
2. knead
3. wreath
4. wrench

5. wrestling
6. rhythm
7. design
8. rhinestone
9. knowledge
10. rhinoceros

Exercise 6

1. wrong   doer
2. wrist   band
3. door   knob
4. knock   out
5. knap   sack
6. ship   wreck
7. knee   pads
8. sign   post
9. sign   board
10. knee   cap

11. wreath
12. signs
13. reigns
14. foreign
15. gnarled
16. knight
17. rhyming
18. wrapping
19. design
20. knit

LESSON | 13

There are more silent letters in this lesson. Some of them have two letters that are exactly the same, and so are known as **double consonants**. Look carefully to see *where* these silent double consonants appear in a word.

SILENT LETTERS AND DOUBLE TROUBLE

EXERCISE 1: EYEBALLING SPELLING LIST 13

Directions: Sweep your eyes across the line from left to right and back again. Do it quickly. Circle the word in each line that looks different from the others on that line.

Are you ready? Get set . . . Go!

1. crams	crumbs	crumbs	crumbs
2. lambs	lambs	lambs	lamps
3. limbs	limps	limbs	limbs
4. spell	spell	shell	spell
5. mess	mess	mess	mist
6. drills	dwells	dwells	dwells
7. winker	wicker	wicker	wicker

8. sticker	sticker	stinker	sticker
9. cracker	cracker	canker	cracker
10. staff	stiff	stiff	stiff

Check your answers with the answer key at the end of this lesson.
My score for Exercise 1 is _____ out of 10.

REFLECTION

Go back to the words that are the same on each line in Exercise 1. Locate the letters *mb, ck, ll, ss,* and *ff.* These letters are partners. When they're together, only one is allowed to speak. In other words, only one out of the two letters represents a sound. You can probably guess the sound of the double letters *ff, ll,* and *ss,* but what sound do the letters *mb* and *ck* represent? You can find out by doing Exercise 2, Sound Inventory.

EXERCISE 2: SOUND INVENTORY

Directions: Listen to yourself as you read each group of words aloud. **You must read the words out loud.** The letters and sounds in each group have something in common. Put a circle around the letters that are the same in each group and then write the two letters on the lines provided.

GROUP 1

bless	staff	drill
mess	cliff	gull
dress	cuff	swell

____ ____ ____

GROUP 2   GROUP 3

comb	rock
tomb	trick
limb	deck

____ ____

In Group 1, the common letters are *ss, ff,* and *ll.* Can you hear the sound of the letters *ss, ff,* and *ll*? Which letters are silent? If you need help, use slash marks to break the words into sounds. The word *bless* should be written as /b/l/e/s/, the word *staff* should be written as /s/t/a/f/, and the word *drill* should be written as /d/r/i/l/. Now can you hear the sounds?

Only one of the double letters makes a sound. The letters *s, f,* and *l* represent the sounds as found in the clue words *sun, fork,* and *lemon.*

In Group 2, the common letters are *mb.* Can you hear the sound of the letters *mb?* Which letter is silent? If you need help, use slash marks to break the words into sounds using the letter/sound strategy. The word *comb* should be written as /c/o/m/ and the word *limb* should be written as /l/i/m/. Now can you hear the sound? The letter *b* is silent and the letter *m* represents the sound as found in the clue word *mailbox.*

In Group 3, the common letters are *ck.* Can you hear the sound of the letters *ck?* Which letter is silent? If you need help, use slash marks to break the words into sounds. The word *rock* should be written as /r/o/k/ and the word *trick* should be written as /t/r/i/k/. Now can you hear the sound? The letter *c* is silent and the letter *k* represents the sound as found in the clue word *key.*

REFLECTION

What consonants did you learn about in this lesson? _____

What sounds do the letters *mb* and *ck* represent? _____

What sounds do the letters *ll* and *ff* and *ss* represent? _____

What can you say about the location of all these double or silent consonants?

_____

_____

The sound /m/, as found in the clue word *mailbox,* is represented by the letters *mb.* The sound /k/, as found in the clue word *key,* is represented by the letters *ck.*

The double letters only make one sound. This means that *ll* sounds like one letter, *l,* as found in the clue word *lemon; ss* is like the letter *s,* as found in the clue word *sun;* and *ff* is like the letter *f,* as found in the clue word *fork.* All of these consonants—double or silent—are located at the end of a word.

EXERCISE 3: PRACTICE SUBSTITUTING WITH ENDING CONSONANTS

Directions: Change the final consonant in each word to *mb, ck, ss, ll,* or *ff.* A few have been done for you. For some words, there is more than one answer.

  1. top   ___*tomb*___   _____   _____   _____

  2. dug   _____   _____   _____

3. nut ___*null*___ _____

4. lap _____ _____ _____

5. gum _____

6. plug _____ _____

7. let _____

8. mix _____ _____

9. pat _____ _____

10. pup ___*puss*___ _____ _____ _____

Check your answers with the answer key at the end of this lesson.

My score for Exercise 3 is _____ out of 10.

EXERCISE 4: PRACTICE WRITING SPELLING LIST 13

Directions: Go back to Exercise 1. Look at the three words that are the same on each line. Write each of these words only once on the lines below. This would be a good time to have your study buddy dictate the words to you.

1. _____   **6.** _____

2. _____   **7.** _____

3. _____   **8.** _____

4. _____   **9.** _____

5. _____   **10.** _____

Consult your dictionary if the meaning of a word is unfamiliar to you.

Check your answers with the answer key at the end of this lesson.

My score for Exercise 4 is _____ out of 10.

EXERCISE 5: PRACTICE WRITING SPELLING LIST 13 IN CONTEXT

Directions: Use the words from Exercise 4 to complete the phrases below. For added practice, rewrite the entire phrase in your own sentence on the provided line.

1. cheese on a _____

_____

2. a _____ basket

_____

3. _____ in a cave

_____

4. _____ on a tablecloth

_____

5. shearing _____ for wool

_____

6. the _____ of a tree

_____

7. _____ the words correctly

_____

8. a parking _____

_____

9. clean up the _____

_____

10. a _____, cramped muscle

_____

Check your answers with the answer key at the end of this lesson. Only the words that go in the blanks are given, since everyone will create different sentences.

My score for Exercise 5 is _____ out of 10.

VARIATIONS

All of the following words contain silent letters, either vowels or consonants. The fact that these letters are silent doesn't mean they don't affect the sound of a word. For instance, without the *u* in *biscuit*, you'd have *biscit*, which, according to the soft *c* rule, would be pronounced /b/i/s/i/t/. The *t* in *listen* gives a different sound than would be heard in *lisen*, which would have a long /i/ sound. This is why it is be said that these silent letters "hold a place."

Read all the words below **aloud.** Look at the bold letters in each word as you say the word. Have your study buddy dictate the words to you while you write them in your notebook.

b**ui**ld	lis**t**en	si**gh**	g**u**ess
bisc**ui**t	fas**t**en	hi**gh**	g**u**ide
mois**t**en	t**h**ou**gh**	g**u**itar	
ske**t**ch	dau**gh**ter		

Do you want more challenging words that contain the *mb, ck, ss, ll,* or *ff* combinations? Try these! Call on your study buddy to dictate them to you as you write them in your notebook. Consult your dictionary if you need to so that you can use the words correctly.

classmate	passkey	guardianship
passbook	password	disguise
grasshopper	guidance	

EXERCISE 6: WHAT HAVE YOU LEARNED?

In Lessons 12 and 13, you learned how silent letters represent no sound but still "hold a place." These silent letters pose a problem when using the letter/sound relationship strategy. Therefore, your memory is your guide. If you have done all the practice exercises diligently, you will have a good chance of spelling the words correctly. This last exercise offers you even more practice. Call upon your study buddy and get to work!

Directions: Read each sentence **aloud.** Circle all the words that have silent letters you learned in Lessons 12 and 13.

1. Listen to the sighs of complaint from that naughty child.
2. The wicker basket will hold wine, cheese, and crackers.
3. The tour guides will present a valid parking sticker to the guard.
4. The plumber will repair the gushing water pipe with a wrench.
5. Moisten the soil and plant the hollyhock seeds.
6. Five new employees have joined the staff at Mill Pass Bank.
7. Use a drill to spell the name on the tombstone.
8. The seagulls dwell by the seashore.
9. The messy table was filled with crumbs from the rhubarb pie.
10. Do you know whether the tree's limbs were destroyed by the lightning storm?

Directions: Read each compound word **aloud.** Then rewrite each compound word as two separate words. These words are loaded with silent letters; see if you can find them all.

11. bombshell _____ _____
12. guardrail _____ _____
13. sketchbook _____ _____
14. guesswork _____ _____

15. highway   _____   _____
16. switchblade   _____   _____
17. guidebook   _____   _____
18. witchcraft   _____   _____
19. thighbone   _____   _____
20. crackerjack   _____   _____

Check your answers with the answer key at the end of this lesson.
My score for Exercise 6 is _____ **out of 20.**

ANSWER KEY FOR LESSON 13

Exercise 1
1. crams
2. lamps
3. limps
4. shell
5. mist
6. drills
7. winker
8. stinker
9. canker
10. staff

Exercise 3
1. tock, toll, toss
2. duck, dull, dumb
3. numb
4. lass, lack, lamb
5. gull
6. pluck, plumb
7. less
8. mill, miss
9. pack, pass
10. pull, puck, puff

Exercise 4
1. crumbs
2. lambs
3. limbs
4. spell
5. mess
6. dwells
7. wicker
8. sticker
9. cracker
10. stiff

Exercise 5
1. cracker
2. wicker
3. dwells
4. crumbs
5. lambs
6. limbs
7. spell
8. sticker
9. mess
10. stiff

Exercise 6

1. listen, sighs, naughty
2. wicker, crackers
3. guides, sticker, guard
4. plumber, wrench
5. moisten, hollyhock
6. staff, Mill, Pass
7. drill, spell, tombstone
8. seagulls, dwell
9. messy, filled, crumbs, rhubarb
10. know, limbs, lightning
11. bomb   shell
12. guard   rail
13. sketch   book
14. guess   work
15. high   way
16. switch   blade
17. guide   book
18. witch   craft
19. thigh   bone
20. cracker   jack

LESSON | 14

You have read the phrase "expand your pool of spelling words" many times in this book. This lesson in particular will help you do this. Take a look at the title. Going from *Expand* to *Expansion* is only a matter of adding a simple ending—*sion*. Once you learn the letter/sound relationship for this ending, learning any number of advanced spelling words will be very simple.

EXPAND... EXPANSION

EXERCISE 1: EYEBALLING SPELLING LIST 14

Directions: Sweep your eyes across the line from left to right and back again. Do it quickly. Circle the word in each line that looks different from the others on that line.

Are you ready? Get set . . . Go!

1. detection	decision	decision	decision
2. depletion	depletion	deletion	depletion
3. perspiration	population	population	population
4. condition	composition	composition	composition
5. inspection	inspection	inspection	inflection
6. evolution	evolution	elocution	evolution
7. imitation	importation	importation	importation

8. vacation	vacation	vaccination	vacation
9. erosion	erosion	erosion	election
10. emotion	emission	emotion	emotion

Check your answers with the answer key at the end of this lesson.
My score for Exercise 1 is _____ out of 10.

REFLECTION

Go back to the words that are the same in each line. Look for the letter *i* near the end of each word. What letters precede (go before) the letter *i*?

_____

The letter *i* is preceded by the letters *t* and *s*. Look for the letters *ti* and *si* in each word; then move on to Exercise 2, Sound Inventory, to hear the sounds these letters represent.

EXERCISE 2: SOUND INVENTORY

Directions: Listen to yourself as you read each group of words aloud. **You must read the words out loud.** The letters and sounds in each group have something in common. Put a circle around the letters that are the same in each group and then write them on the lines provided.

GROUP 1
mansion
pension
expansion

____

GROUP 2
action
nation
motion

____

In Group 1, the common letters are *sion.* Can you hear the sound of the letters *sion?* If not, use slash marks to break the words into sounds. The word *mansion* is represented by the sounds /m/a/n/sh/u/n/. The letters *si* sound like /sh/, as found in the clue word **shake**. Now can you hear the sound? The letters *sion* represent the sound /sh/u/n/.

In Group 2, the common letters are *tion.* Can you hear the sound of the letters *tion?* If not, use slash marks to break the words into sounds. The word *nation* is represented by the sounds /n/a/sh/u/n/. The letters *ti* sound like /sh/, as found in the clue word **shake**. Now can you hear the sound? The letters *tion* represent the sound /sh/u/n/.

REFLECTION

What letters represent the sound of /sh/? _____

What sounds do the letters *sion* and *tion* represent? _____

Which letters represent the ending that sounds like the word *shun?*

_____

The English language chooses to use the letters *si* and *ti* to represent the sound of /sh/. The letters *tion* and *sion* represent the ending that sounds like *shun.*

Move on to Exercise 3 to practice spelling words with the endings *tion* and *sion.*

EXERCISE 3: THE EXPANSION OF WORDS

Directions: Each of the following words is written as it sounds. Write each word with its correct spelling. The /sh/ sound is represented by the letters *ti.* The first word has been done for you.

1. /p/o/p/u/l/a/sh/u/n/   *population*
2. /e/d/u/c/a/sh/u/n/
3. /c/o/m/m/u/n/i/c/a/sh/u/n/
4. /l/o/c/a/sh/u/n/
5. /i/m/i/t/a/sh/u/n/
6. /c/o/m/p/l/e/sh/u/n/
7. /e/k/s/p/ir/a/sh/u/n/
8. /i/n/v/e/n/sh/un/
9. /a/d/o/p/sh/u/n/
10. /i/n/v/e/s/t/i/g/a/sh/u/n/
11. /e/k/s/p/or/t/a/sh/u/n/
12. /d/e/p/or/t/a/sh/u/n/
13. /v/i/s/i/t/a/sh/u/n/
14. /o/b/s/er/v/a/sh/u/n/
15. /e/k/s/p/l/a/n/a/sh/u/n/
16. /i/n/s/t/i/t/u/sh/u/n/
17. /t/a/k/s/a/sh/u/n/
18. /i/n/s/er/sh/u/n/
19. /au/t/o/m/a/sh/u/n/
20. /e/kw/a/sh/u/n/

Directions: Each of the following words is written as it sounds. Write each word with the correct spelling. The /sh/ sound is represented by the letters *si.*

21. /s/u/s/p/e/n/sh/u/n/   _____

22. /e/k/s/p/a/n/sh/u/n/   _____

23. /m/a/n/sh/u/n/   _____

24. /l/e/sh/u/n/   _____

Check your answers with the answer key at the end of this lesson.

My score for Exercise 3 is _____ out of 24.

EXERCISE 4: PRACTICE WRITING SPELLING LIST 14

Directions: Go back to Exercise 1. Look at the three words that are the same on each line. Write each of these words only once on the lines below. This would be a good time to have your study buddy dictate the words to you.

1. _____

2. _____

3. _____

4. _____

5. _____

6. _____

7. _____

8. _____

9. _____

10. _____

Consult your dictionary if the meaning of a word is unfamiliar to you.

Check your answers with the answer key at the end of this lesson.

My score for Exercise 4 is _____ out of 10.

EXERCISE 5: PRACTICE WRITING SPELLING LIST 14 IN CONTEXT

1. _____ from abroad

   _____

2. a two-week _____

   _____

3. soil _____

   _____

4. a jury's _____

   _____

5. _____ of oil and gasoline

   _____

6. your car's _____ sticker

_____

7. dense _____ in the city

_____

8. humanity's _____ through time

_____

9. a 500-word _____

_____

10. the _____ of love

_____

Check your answers with the answer key at the end of this lesson. Only the words that go in the blanks are given, since everyone will create different sentences.

My score for Exercise 5 is _____ out of 10.

VARIATIONS

Some words double the letter *s*. In those words, the sound of /sh/u/n/ is represented by the letters *ssion*. Below are some examples.

mission	omission	emission	permission
commission	admission	transmission	depression
expression	impression	compression	concussion
percussion	discussion	session	passion

The following words also have the letters *si*, but these letters represent the combined sound of /z/ and /h/, as found in the Consonant Key. In these words, the *si* makes a sort of vibrating sound. You can hear it clearly in the word *television* and words like these.

vision	provision	supervision	fusion
confusion	transfusion	illusion	conclusion
precision	erosion		

 Do you want more challenging words with the /sh/u/n/ sound? Try these! Call on your study buddy to dictate them to you as you write them in your notebook.

classification	participation	equalization	nationalization
affirmation	defamation	instituion	mummification
constitution	restitution	rendition	organization
oration			

EXERCISE 6: WHAT HAVE YOU LEARNED?

Directions: Select one word in parenthesis to correctly complete each sentence.

1. The financial _____ offers instant cash access. (institute, institution)

2. The pamphlet will provide an _____ of the health benefits. (explain, explanation)

3. The sales person will receive a two-week _____. (vacate, vacation)

4. Did you receive the order _____ by e-mail? (confirmation, confirm)

5. There is no _____ from the customer-service link. (communicate, communication)

6. The credit card will offer retail _____ service. (protect, protection)

7. _____ of the computer will be by an authorized dealer. (Install, Installation)

8. The _____ date is stamped on every bottle of soda. (expire, expiration)

9. The claims will be processed after the _____. (invest, investigation)

10. Mail _____ is a service provided by the United States Post Office. (collect, collection)

Check your answers with the answer key at the end of this lesson.
My score for Exercise 6 is _____ out of 10.

Once you've finished filling in the blanks, read each sentence aloud. Call on your study buddy to dictate the sentences to you. They're challenging, but you can do it!

ANSWER KEY FOR LESSON 14

Exercise 1

1. detection
2. deletion
3. perspiration
4. condition
5. inflection
6. elocution
7. imitation
8. vaccination
9. election
10. emission

Exercise 3

1. population
2. education
3. communication
4. location
5. imitation
6. completion
7. expiration
8. invention
9. adoption
10. investigation
11. exportation
12. deportation
13. visitation
14. observation
15. explanation
16. institution
17. taxation
18. insertion
19. automation
20. equation
21. suspension
22. expansion
23. mansion
24. lesion

Exercise 4

1. decision
2. depletion
3. population
4. composition
5. inspection
6. evolution
7. importation
8. vacation
9. erosion
10. emotion

Exercise 5

1. importation
2. vacation
3. erosion
4. decision
5. depletion
6. inspection
7. population
8. evolution
9. composition
10. emotion

Exercise 6

1. institution
2. explanation
3. vacation
4. confirmation
5. communication
6. protection
7. installation
8. expiration
9. investigation
10. collection

LESSON | 15

BEAT THE STRESS

This lesson is about the rhythm of words. Rhythm is the musical quality of words caused by the "beats" you hear in a word and how these beats are stressed or accented. These beats are called **syllables**. Spelling will be easier when you learn to write words beat by beat or syllable by syllable. Doesn't that sound rhythmical?

EXERCISE 1: EYEBALLING SPELLING LIST 15

Directions: Sweep your eyes across the line from left to right and back again. Do it quickly. Circle the word in each line that looks different from the others on that line.

Are you ready? Get set . . . Go!

1. sparkles	sparklers	sparklers	sparklers
2. slippery	sloppy	slippery	slippery
3. labeling	labeling	label	labeling
4. robbery	robberies	robberies	robberies
5. music	musical	musical	musical
6. desert	deserting	deserting	deserting
7. batteries	battery	battery	battery

129

8. billowing	billowed	billowing	billowing
9. happier	happy	happier	happier
10. projected	projected	project	projected

Check your answers with the answer key at the end of this lesson.
My score for Exercise 1 is _____ out of 10.

REFLECTION

Go back to the words that are different on each line. Compare them to the three identical words. What sets the odd words apart in rows 1–10?

_____

What endings do you see? _____

_____

The words are almost the same on each line, except for the endings. You should have found *ed, ier, ing, y, al, ies,* and *ers.* These are all endings that give the main word an added beat or two. They are **syllables**. A syllable can be either a consonant and a vowel or a vowel alone. Move on to Exercise 2, Sound Inventory, to fully hear the beats or syllables in a word.

EXERCISE 2: SOUND INVENTORY

Directions: Follow the arrows from left to right as you read the following lines of words. Read each line **aloud** or have your study buddy read them to you. This time, listen for the number of beats or syllables in each word and write the number of beats you hear on the provided space. For example, the word *hum* has one syllable. The word *hummer* has two syllables. *Hummingbird* has three syllables. You try it.

1. ham	_1_	hammer	_2_	hammering	_3_
2. slip	_1_	slipper	____	slippery	____
3. rob	____	robber	____	robberies	____
4. visit	____	visited	____	visitation	____
5. limit	____	limited	____	limitation	____

Check your answers with the answer key at the end of this lesson.
My score for Exercise 2 is _____ out of 15 (three answers on a line).

For numbers 1–3, the first word in the line had 1 syllable, the next word across had 2 syllables, and the final word on the line had 3 syllables.

Do you see that every syllable has a vowel? Separate the syllables in your mind as you say the word **aloud** before you try to spell any word on paper. You have just acquired another spelling strategy—spelling the words syllable by syllable.

Move on to the next part of Sound Inventory to identify the first vowel in each syllable.

Directions: Read each of the following groups of words aloud. Listen very carefully to the vowel (the second sound) in the first syllable. Which group has the short vowel and which group has the long vowel sounds in the first syllable? Write the word *long* or *short* on the line below the group.

If you need help recalling the sounds of the vowels, refer to the Letter/Sound Relationship Key in the introduction.

GROUP 1   ## GROUP 2

lim	it	mi	ser
ped	al	tu	lip
sav	age	la	bel
mod	el	de	mon
pun	ish	clo	ver

____   ____

Group 1 has a short vowel in the first syllable. When a vowel sits between two consonants, the sound is usually short. This also can be called a **closed syllable**.

Group 2 has a long vowel in the first syllable. When a vowel ends the syllable, the sound is usually long. This also can be called an **open syllable.**

EXERCISE 3: SOUND AND MEANING

You need to know the following general rule about vowels in open and closed syllables, because changing the stress, or accent, in a word can change a syllable from open to closed or vice versa. This change leads to a change in the sound—and meaning—of a word.

Look at these two words:

mi nute´   min´ ute

They are spelled exactly the same but are written with spaces between them to denote syllables. The first word has an **open syllable** and the other has a **closed syllable.** Thus, the first vowel sound is different in each word.

Some syllables are emphasized more than others in a word. This is called **stress**. Stress can bounce from syllable to syllable. The dictionary uses an accent mark (´), to show which syllable is stressed or emphasized when spoken aloud. The vowel in a stressed syllable can either be long or short.

Say the following two words aloud:

    mi nute´   min´ ute

In the first word, the first syllable has a long vowel /i/ and the second syllable is stressed. In the second word, the first syllable has a short vowel /i/ and the first syllable is stressed. Read the following sentences to help you pronounce the two words correctly.

The detective asked the witness for even the minute (mi nute´) details of the robbery.

The fax will be sent in a minute (min´ ute) or two.

You should have figured out by now that changing the stress also can change the meaning of a word. There are many words like this, and the letter/sound relationship strategy holds true for all of them. If you write what you hear, you will have no problem.

Directions: Practice hearing the stress by reading the following words. You will see that the stress bounces from first to second syllable as you move down the list. Read the pairs of words and write whether the first vowel is long or short. Read the sentences **aloud** to help you.

WORD   **VOWEL**

1. re   fuse´   <u> long /e/ </u>

The Automated Teller Machine refused to accept the debit card.

2. ref´ use   <u> short /e/ </u>

Financial Institutions are inundated with paper. Who will cart the refuse away?

3. min´ ute   <u>   </u>

The laser printer prints 50 pages each minute and 100 pages in two minutes.

4. mi   nute´   <u>   </u>

The shredder cut the paper into minute pieces.

5. rec´ ord   _____

The paper receipt is a record of the sales transaction.

6. re cord´   _____

A camcorder will record your memories on tape.

7. proj´ ect   _____

On-line customer service is a project for this new company.

8. pro ject´   _____

What do you project will be the expandability of this compute system?

Check your answers with the answer key at the end of this lesson.

My score for Exercise 3 is _____ out of 8.

REFLECTION

What is the musical quality in a word called? _____

What are the beats in a word called? _____

How will the syllables strategy help the speller? _____

_____

What can you say about the vowel sound in a closed syllable?

_____

What can you say about the vowel sound in an open syllable?

_____

What happens if the stress changes in a word? _____

_____

The musical quality of a word is called **rhythm.** The beats you hear are called **syllables.** Spelling can be made easier by writing what you hear, syllable by syllable. The vowel in an open syllable, like the syllable *mi* in the word *mi nute,* is usually a long sound. The vowel in a closed syllable, like the syllable *min* in the word *min ute,* is usually a short sound. A syllable can be emphasized or stressed. When the stress changes in the same word, it also changes its meaning.

By now you should be very comfortable with the letter/sound relationship strategy and be quite aware that there are exceptions to this strategy. This holds true for the vowels. A vowel can lose its long or short sound to something called a **schwa.** This happens in multi-syllable words and is represented by an upside down letter *e.* When a vowel sounds like the vowel in the word *of,* that vowel is said to have a schwa sound. Any vowel, *a, e, i, o, u,* or *y,* can lose its original sound to a schwa. The following are a few words that have the vowel as a schwa sound. The bold vowel is the schwa.

doct**o**r	com**a**tose	ign**o**ramus	inf**a**ntile
ch**a**uvinism	lucr**a**tive	medioc**r**e	neighb**o**r

Any vowel can be represented by the schwa sound, so at times the letter/sound relationship can be difficult. The schwa sound will appear again in the following lessons.

EXERCISE 4: PRACTICE WRITING SPELLING LIST 15

Directions: Go back to Exercise 1. Look at the three words that are the same on each line. Write each of these words only once on the lines below. This would be a good time to have your study buddy dictate the words to you.

1. _____   6. _____

2. _____   7. _____

3. _____   8. _____

4. _____   9. _____

5. _____   10. _____

Consult your dictionary if the meaning of a word is unfamiliar to you.

Check your answers with the answer key at the end of this lesson.

My score for Exercise 4 is _____ out of 10.

EXERCISE 5: PRACTICE WRITING SPELLING LIST 15 IN CONTEXT

Directions: Use the words from Exercise 4 to complete the phrases below. For added practice, rewrite the entire phrase in your own sentence on the provided line.

1. a _____, waxed floor

_____

2. a _____ play on Broadway

_____

3. police reports about _____

_____

4. _____ the army for freedom

_____

5. _____ clouds of smoke

_____

6. _____ future plans

_____

7. _____ the food products

_____

8. a car _____

_____

9. a _____, friendlier person

_____

10. _____ for the 4th of July

_____

Check your answers with the answer key at the end of this lesson. Only the words that go in the blanks are given, since everyone will create different sentences.

My score for Exercise 5 is _____ out of 10.

VARIATIONS

In Lesson 3, you learned about two-vowel combinations that represent one sound. For example, the word *sea* (meaning the ocean) has two vowels, but the letters *ea* represent only one sound—long /e/. This is not always the case with two vowels together. Sometimes, when words are broken into syllables between the two vowels, both letters are pronounced. In this case, the first syllable is open and the second syllable begins with a vowel. For example, the word *diet* has two vowels, but the word *diet* also has two syllables. Read the word *diet* as /d/i/ /e/t/. Read the following words syllable by syllable.

po em	po et
ri ot	ru in
tri o	vid e o

Another syllable to look closely at is **consonant + *le***. The final letter *e* is silent. Examples of the consonant + *le* syllable include the letters *ble*, as found in the word *table* (/t/a/b/l/); *cle* as found in the word *circle* (/s/ir/c/l/); *dle*, as found in the word *handle* (/h/a/n/d/l/); *kle*, as found in the word *ankle* (/a/n/k/l/); *ple*, as found in the word *people* (/p/e/p/l/);

and *tle*, as found in the word *title* (/t/i/t/l/). Just remember that with the consonant + *le* relationship, the letter/sound relationship is consistent and the final letter *e* is silent. The following are a few more words to illustrate this syllable.

sparkle purple

stable little

candle gargle

Note that if you add the letter *r*, as in the word *sparkler*, the letters *er* together make the murmur vowel /er/ so that the *e* is no longer silent.

 Spelling words that end in *able* or *ible* can be challenging because both endings sound the same. The *a* in *able* and the *i* in *ible* both have the schwa sound, the sound you hear in the word *of*. Try these *able* and *ible* words if you're ready for the challenge. Call on your study buddy to dictate them to you as you write them in your notebook.

payable	accountable	expandable	profitable
advisable	inevitable	perishable	attainable
transferable	inexcusable		

responsible	deductible	convertible	compatible
sensible	eligible		

EXERCISE 6: WHAT HAVE YOU LEARNED?

Directions: Separate the words into syllables and write whether the vowel in the first syllable is long or short. The first one is done for you.

WORD	SYLLABLES	FIRST VOWEL
1. slippery	slip per y	short /i/
2. dragon	_____	_____
3. clever	_____	_____
4. bacon	_____	_____
5. robberies	_____	_____
6. vanish	_____	_____
7. silently	_____	_____
8. buttery	_____	_____
9. musical	_____	_____
10. billowing	_____	_____

Directions: Write all the words in the following sentences that have three syllables. For added practice, have your study buddy dictate the sentences to you.

11. Billowing clouds were sparkling in the sunset.
12. The buttery popcorn slipped from her hands.
13. The shimmering desert sun beat endlessly on the arid sand.
14. The recording studio projected a profit of three million dollars.
15. The financial advisor hammered out all the minute details of the contract.
16. Mr. Butterly, the project manager, refused to take the blame for the stolen batteries.
17. The musical interlude prepared us for happier moments.
18. The people waited for the jury's decision.
19. The police reported no robberies for a period of two weeks.
20. Let's celebrate Independence Day with sparklers and fire works.

Check your answers with the answer key at the end of this lesson.
My score for Exercise 6 is _____ out of 10.

ANSWER KEY FOR LESSON 15
Exercise 1

1. sparkles
2. sloppy
3. label
4. robbery
5. music
6. desert
7. batteries
8. billowed
9. happy
10. project

Exercise 2

1. 1,2,3
2. 1,2,3
3. 1,2,3

4. 2,3,4
5. 2,3,4

Exercise 3

1. long /e/
2. short /e/
3. short /i/
4. long /i/
5. short /e/
6. long /e/
7. short /o/
8. long /o/

Exercise 4

1. sparklers
2. slippery
3. labeling
4. robberies
5. musical
6. deserting
7. battery
8. billowing
9. happier
10. projected

Exercise 5

1. slippery
2. musical
3. robberies
4. deserting
5. billowing
6. projected
7. labeling
8. battery
9. happier
10. sparklers

Exercise 6

1. slip per y   short /i/
2. drag on   short /a/
3. clev er   short /e/
4. ba con   long /a/
5. rob ber ies   short /o/
6. van ish   short /a/
7. si lent ly   long /i/
8. but ter y   short /u/
9. mu si cal   long /u/
10. bil low ing   short /i/
11. billowing (sparkling is actually only two syllables— spar kling)
12. buttery
13. shimmering, endlessly
14. recording, studio, projected
15. financial, advisor
16. Butterly, manager, batteries
17. musical, interlude, happier
18. decision
19. reported, robberies
20. celebrate, fireworks

LESSON | 16

This lesson focuses on the ever-changing base word. As you know, a foundation is something you can build on—and that is exactly what you will do in this lesson as you learn how to build on the base, or foundation, word.

THE BASE WORD

EXERCISE 1: EYEBALLING SPELLING LIST 16

Directions: Sweep your eyes across the line from left to right and back again. Do it quickly. Circle the word in each line that looks different from the others on that line.

Are you ready? Get set . . . Go!

1. wanted	waited	waited	waited
2. composed	composed	composed	compiled
3. touched	torched	touched	touched
4. debts	debits	debits	debits
5. taxable	taxes	taxes	taxes
6. bunches	bunches	brunches	bunches
7. paging	paying	paging	paging

8. submitting   submitting   subletting   submitting
9. shipped   shipped   shipped   shopped
10. cashing   clashing   cashing   cashing

Check your answers with the answer key at the end of this lesson.
My score for Exercise 1 is _____ out of 10.

REFLECTION

Go back to the words that are the same in each line. Find the base or foundation word. Now look at the endings attached to each base word. Write all the endings that you see. _____
Why do you think the words have different endings? _____
_____

If you noticed that the words ended with *ing, ed, es,* and *s,* that's a great start. The words have different endings for a very good reason. Words are usually said or written in context (sentences) that convey meaning. When a word is about an action, the ending of the base word informs the listener or reader about when something is happening. The ending conveys the **tense** (time) of the verb (action word). The tense could be the past (yesterday or last year), present (going on right now), or the future (tomorrow or years from now). It is the base word that conveys the **meaning** and the end that conveys the sense of **when** the base word happened. Keep your eye on the base words *step* and *fax* in the following sentences:

She **steps** on the rocks.   He **faxes** the information.
She is **stepping** on the rocks.   He **faxed** the information.
She **stepped** on the rocks.   He is **faxing** the information.

Can you see and hear how the base word changes?
If the base word refers to a thing—that is, if the base word is a noun—the ending can change to indicate the "number of," or the amount. If the amount is one, it's called **singular,** and if the amount is more than one, it's called **plural.** Keep your eye on the base words *battery, box,* and *label* in the following sentences.

The small radio needs one **battery**, but the larger radio needs
six **batteries.**
Put all the paper in one **box** and the rest of the materials in several
larger **boxes.**
Each folder will get one red **label** and three yellow **labels.**

Can you see and hear how the base word changes?

This is all you need to know for now. Move on to Exercise 2, Sound
Inventory, to hear the sounds of these endings so you can continue
improving your spelling.

EXERCISE 2: SOUND INVENTORY

Directions: Listen to yourself as you read each group of words aloud. **You
must read the words out loud.** The letters and sounds in each group
have something in common. Put a circle around the letters that are the
same in each group and then write the two letters on the lines provided.

GROUP 1

waited	filed	jumped
planted	climbed	spiked
loaded	mailed	liked
rented	curved	danced
lasted	thanked	
	shaved	

____

GROUP 2

brushes	boxes
dishes	taxes
wishes	buzzes
lunches	classes
speeches	passes

____

In Group 1, the common letters are *ed.* Can you hear the sound of the
letters *ed?* Group 1 has three sets of words ending with the letters *ed.*
That's because the letters *ed* can represent three different sounds. Break
all the words into sounds using slash marks. The word *lasted* should look
like /l/a/s/t/e/d/. The word *jumped* should look like /j/u/m/p/t/, and the
word *filed* should look like /f/i/l/d/. Can you hear that the letters *ed* represent the sound of /e/d/, /t/, and /d/? The *ed* is used to change the tense of
a base word to indicate that an action took place in the past.

In Group 2, the common letters are *es.* Can you hear the sound of the
letters *es?* Break all the words in Group 2 into sounds using slash marks.
The word *brushes* should look like /b/r/u/sh/e/s/ and the word *boxes*

should look like /b/o/k/s/e/s/. Now can you hear the sound? Remember this general rule:

The tense and number of words ending with *ch, sh, s, x,* and *z* is changed by adding the letters *es* to the end of the word.

Other words just take on the letter *s* as part of the letter/sound relationship when they change tense or number. Using slash marks, the word *label* looks like /l/a/b/l/, and labels looks like /la/b/l/s/.

The rules aren't a necessary part of this lesson as long as you keep the letter/sound relationship. You heard that the letters *ed* can sound like /e/d/, /t/, or /d/. You heard /s/ and /e/s/. Keep spelling syllable by syllable and you will keep expanding your pool of spelling words.

REFLECTION
Why does a word have an ending? _____

_____

What letters in this lesson represent tense? _____
What letters in this lesson so far mean the number of or the amount?

_____

The letters *ed* can represent three sounds. What are the sounds?

_____

Endings for words used to indicate tense—past, present, or future— are the letters *s, es, ed,* and *ing*. The number amount—singular or plural—is indicated by the endings *s* and *es*. The letters *ed* represent the sounds /d/, /t/, and /e/d/ (like the male nickname Ed). Move on to Exercise 3 to practice listening for ending sounds.

EXERCISE 3: PRACTICE WITH ENDINGS
Directions: Read each word aloud. Listen carefully for the sound at the end of the word. Write the symbol /d/, /t/, or /e/d/ for the sound you hear. The first few are done for you. Get your study buddy to read the words to you. Try to really focus your listening.

1. depleted _/e/d/_	**6.** uplifted ____	**11.** touched ____
2. ordered _/d/_	**7.** landed ____	**12.** played ____
3. thanked _/t/_	**8.** served ____	**13.** wished ____
4. raced ____	**9.** rented ____	**14.** waited ____
5. composed ____	**10.** sounded ____	**15.** printed ____

Check your answers with the answer key at the end of this lesson.
My score for Exercise 3 is _____ out of 15.

Now try a practice exercise that will sharpen your spelling of endings.
Directions: Read the words **aloud** from left to right. Practice writing the words or call on your study buddy to dictate the words to you. It's a good idea to listen syllable by syllable before you write.

touch	touches	touched	touching
buzz	buzzes	buzzed	buzzing
punch	punches	punched	punching
brush	brushes	brushed	brushing
fax	faxes	faxed	faxing
flex	flexes	flexed	flexing
retail	retails	retailed	retailing
page	pages	paged	paging

EXERCISE 4: PRACTICE WRITING SPELLING LIST 16

Directions: Go back to Exercise 1. Look at the three words that are the same on each line. Write each of these words only once on the lines below. This would be a good time to have your study buddy dictate the words to you.

1. _____   6. _____
2. _____   7. _____
3. _____   8. _____
4. _____   9. _____
5. _____   10. _____

Consult your dictionary if the meaning of a word is unfamiliar to you.
Check your answers with the answer key at the end of this lesson.
My score for Exercise 4 is _____ out of 10.

EXERCISE 5: PRACTICE WRITING SPELLING LIST 16 IN CONTEXT

Directions: Use the words from Exercise 4 to complete the following phrases. For added practice, rewrite the entire phrase in your own sentence on the provided line.

1. _____ your partner on the intercom

   _____

2. _____ at the bus stop

   _____

3. your check _____

   _____

4. _____ via overnight delivery

   _____

5. _____ to your request

   _____

6. _____ on the bank statement

   _____

7. _____ of fragrant flowers

   _____

8. pay city and state _____

   _____

9. _____ music for the lyrics

   _____

10. _____ the soft, silky fabric

   _____

Check your answers with the answer key at the end of this lesson. Only the words that go in the blanks are given, since everyone will create different sentences.

My score for Exercise 5 is _____ out of 10.

VARIATIONS

Here are the variations of some words when changing them from singular (one) to plural (many).

Some words that end in *f* or *fe* change the *f* or *fe* to the letter *v* and add the letters *es*.

leaf	leaves	calf	calves
loaf	loaves	half	halves
thief	thieves	shelf	shelves

Some words that end in the vowel *o* add the letter *s* if the *o* is preceded by a vowel, or the letters *es* if the *o* is preceded by a consonant.

radio	radios	patio	patios
rodeo	rodeos	tomato	tomatoes
potato	potatoes	echo	echoes
zero	zeroes	veto	vetoes
duo	duos	igloo	igloos

Some words that end with a consonant plus the letter *y* change the *y* to *i* and add *es*.

lily	lilies	cherry	cherries
pony	ponies	penny	pennies

Some words that end with a vowel followed by the letter *y* simply take the letter *s*.

key	keys	tray	trays
day	days	turkey	turkeys

The final consonant in the base word is sometimes doubled, as in the next group of words.

submit	submitted	submitting
ship	shipped	shipping

The letter/sound relationship doesn't always work when the base word receives an ending. Take out your notebook and practice the words below. Write them many times or in sentences.

 Do you want to see more challenging words in different tenses? Try these! Call on your study buddy to dictate them to you as you write them in your notebook.

copy	notify	erode
copies	notifies	erodes
copied	notified	eroded
copying	notifying	eroding
copier	notification	erosion
nod	vary	permit
nods	varies	permits
nodded	varied	permitted
nodding	variation	permission

EXERCISE 6: WHAT HAVE YOU LEARNED?

Directions: Choose a word that best completes the sentence. For added practice, ask your study buddy to dictate the completed sentences to you. Write them in your notebook.

1. How many _____ will you attend next semester? (class, classes)
2. He _____ the lyrics in the twilight of his life. (composes, composed)
3. The pansies _____ in the garden all summer. (blooms, bloomed)
4. Paying city and state _____ is your responsibility. (taxes, taxed)
5. Chop two _____ of parsley for that salad. (bunches, bunched)
6. The orders were _____ two weeks ago. (submit, submitted)
7. The toddler climbed the _____ and sang a song. (steps, stepping)
8. The team _____ two hours for the rain to stop. (waited, waiting)
9. The gardener planted rose _____ along the slate path. (bush, bushes)
10. The baker removed five _____ of bread from the brick oven. (loaf, loaves)

Check your answers with the answer key at the end of this lesson.
My score for Exercise 6 is _____ out of 10.

ANSWER KEY FOR LESSON 16

Exercise 1
1. wanted
2. compiled
3. torched
4. debts
5. taxable
6. brunches
7. paying
8. subletting
9. shopped
10. clashing

Exercise 3
1. /e/d/
2. /d/
3. /t/
4. /t/
5. /d/
6. /e/d/
7. /e/d/
8. /d/
9. /e/d/
10. /e/d/
11. /t/
12. /d/
13. /t/
14. /e/d/
15. /e/d/

Exercise 4
1. waited
2. composed
3. touched

4. debits
5. taxes
6. bunches
7. paging
8. submitting
9. shipped
10. cashing

Exercise 5
1. paging
2. waited
3. cashing
4. shipped
5. submitting
6. debits
7. bunches
8. taxes
9. composed
10. touched

Exercise 6
1. classes
2. composed
3. bloomed
4. taxes
5. bunches
6. submitted
7. steps
8. waited
9. bushes
10. loaves

LESSON | 17

New words can be derived from a base word, also known as the **root** word, by adding syllables. Syllables that have a specific meaning are called **prefixes** and **suffixes**. This lesson shows you how to add prefixes and suffixes to base words to further increase your pool of spelling words.

GETTING OFF FIRST BASE

EXERCISE 1: EYEBALLING SPELLING LIST 17

Directions: Sweep your eyes across the line from left to right and back again. Do it quickly. Circle the word in each line that looks different from the others on that line.

Are you ready? Get set . . . Go!

1. reaction	retraction	reaction	reaction
2. overpasses	overpass	overpass	overpass
3. pretesting	pretesting	pretesting	presenting
4. unbreakable	unspeakable	unbreakable	unbreakable
5. interview	interviewer	interviewer	interviewer
6. impure	impolite	impolite	impolite
7. disgraceful	disgraceful	distrustful	disgraceful

8. mistreatment	mistreatment	mistreatment	misstatement
9. informative	instructive	informative	informative
10. impossible	impassable	impassable	impassable

Check your answers with the answer key at the end of this lesson.
My score for Exercise 1 is _____ out of 10.

REFLECTION

Go back to the words that are the same in each line. Look at the words very carefully. Remove a syllable at the beginning of each word and remove a syllable at the end of each word. Now look at what's left. The remaining word is called a *base*, or *root*, word. The base word is *act* in the word *reaction*. Try to locate all the other base words.

In the word *unbreakable*, there is a base word, a prefix, and a suffix.

$$\textit{un (prefix)} + \textit{break (base)} + \textit{able (suffix)}$$

You'll learn more about prefixes and suffixes later in this lesson.

Move on to Exercise 2, Sound Inventory, to listen for common base words.

EXERCISE 2: SOUND INVENTORY

Directions: Read each group of words **aloud** and listen for the base word in each group. Write the base word on the line below each group.

GROUP 1
reaction
inaction
interaction
_____

GROUP 2
uncover
recovery
discover
_____

GROUP 3
exportation
transportation
export
_____

GROUP 4
publication
republication
publicly
_____

GROUP 5
enjoyable
joyous
joyful
_____

The base word in Group 1 is *act*. There are three prefixes: *re, in,* and *inter.* The prefixes are spelled exactly as you would expect from the letter/sound relationship.

There is one suffix: *ion*. The letters *ion* represent the sound /sh/u/n/, as you learned in Lesson 14. So, the word *reaction*, represented in sounds, is written as /r/e/a/c/sh/u/n/.

The base word in Group 2 is *cover*. There are three prefixes: *un, re,* and *dis*. The suffix is *y*. The prefixes are spelled exactly as you would expect from the letter/sound relationship. So the word *discovery*, represented as sounds, is written as /d/i/s/c/o/v/er/y/.

The base word in Group 3 is *port*. There are two prefixes: *ex* and *trans*. The prefixes are spelled exactly as you would expect from the letter/sound relationship. There is one suffix: *ation*, which is represented in sounds as /a/sh/u/n/. So the word *exportation*, represented in sounds, is written as /e/k/s/p/or/t/a/sh/u/n/.

The base word in Group 4 is *public*. There is one prefix: *re*. There are two suffixes: *ation*, represented as /a/sh/u/n/, and *ly*, represented as /l/e/, as found in the letter/sound relationship. So the word *republication*, represented by sounds, is written as /r/e/p/u/b/l/i/c/a/sh/u/n/.

The base word in Group 5 is *joy*. There is one prefix: *en*. There are three suffixes: *ful*, which is spelled exactly as you would expect from the letter/sound relationship; and *ous*, represented as /u/s/; and *able*, represented as /a/b/l/. Therefore, the word *joyous*, represented in sounds, is written /j/oy/u/s/, and the word *enjoyable* is written as /e/n/j/oy/a/b/l/. The vowels in *able* and *ous* lose their sound to schwa. (See Lesson 15.)

The syllables added to the beginning of the words are called **prefixes.** They influence the base word because they have meaning. The following is a list of prefixes and their meanings, with clue phrases to help you remember their meanings.

Prefix	Meaning	Clue Phrase
re	to do again	retesting students
pre	before	pretest results
mis	wrong or bad	misspell words
mid	middle of	midnight snack
ir	not/opposite of	irrational behavior
im	not/opposite of	impossible tasks
un	not/opposite of	unhappy gamblers
in	not/into	inactive stocks
il	not/opposite of	illegal handguns
inter	among, between	interactive groups

The syllable added to the end of a word is called a **suffix.** Like the prefix, it also adds to the meaning of a base word.

Prefix	Meaning	Clue Phrase
ful	full of	joyful
less	without, free from	careless
ly	how something is done	expertly
y	tells what something is like	rocky
en	what something is made of	golden
able	tells what something can do or be	passable
ous	full of or like	dangerous
ism	act or fact of doing	criticism
ible	what something can do or be	responsible

Endings, highlighted in bold below, change a base word to a derivative form.

Base	Derivative Form	Letter/Sound Relationship
elect	elect**ion**	/sh/u/n/
examine	examina**tion**	/a/sh/u/n/
sculpt	sculp**ture**	/ch/ur/
depend	depend**ence**	/e/n/s/ (schwa vowel)
assist	assist**ance**	/a/n/s/ (schwa vowel)
dismiss	dismiss**al**	/a/l/ (schwa vowel)

Prefixes and Suffixes Are Consistent

It's important to remember that most prefixes and suffixes are consistent with the letter/sound relationship strategy. The words you'll be spelling from here on in are multi-syllabled, but don't worry, you have the skills to do it. Just spell words beat by beat, syllable by syllable.

REFLECTION

What can be attached to the beginning and ending of a base word to change its meaning? _____

No matter how many letters long the word is, why will you still be able to spell it correctly? _____

_____

Prefixes and suffixes can be added to a base word to change its meaning. No matter how complex the word is that you're trying to spell, you will be successful. Why? You know about letter/sound relationships, and prefixes and suffixes usually follow this strategy. Always listen syllable by syllable before you attempt to spell a word.

EXERCISE 3: PRACTICE WITH BASE WORDS

Directions: Read each word **aloud** and write the base word on the provided line.

1. overpass _____   6. impassable _____
2. replacement _____   7. unreasonable _____
3. impoliteness _____   8. distrustfu _____
4. unmanageable _____   9. reaction _____
5. interviewers _____   10. mistreatment _____

Check your answers with the answer key at the end of this lesson.
My score for Exercise 3 is _____ out of 10.

EXERCISE 4: PRACTICE WRITING SPELLING LIST 17

Directions: Go back to Exercise 1. Look at the three words that are the same on each line. Write each of these words only once on the lines below. This would be a good time to have your study buddy dictate the words to you.

1. _____   6. _____
2. _____   7. _____
3. _____   8. _____
4. _____   9. _____
5. _____   10. _____

Consult your dictionary if the meaning of a word is unfamiliar to you.
    Check your answers with the answer key at the end of this lesson.
My score for Exercise 4 is _____ out of 10.

EXERCISE 5: PRACTICE WRITING SPELLING LIST 17 IN CONTEXT

Directions: Use the words from Exercise 4 to complete the phrases below. For added practice, rewrite the entire phrase in your own sentence on the provided line.

1. a talk-show _____

2. an allergic _____

_____

3. _____ of the prisoners

_____

4. an _____, icy highway

_____

5. _____ for a diagnosis

_____

6. _____ plastic dishes

_____

7. the _____ crosses the highway

_____

8. _____ behavior in front of the family

_____

9. an _____ textbook

_____

10. _____ and without manners

_____

Check your answers with the answer key at the end of this lesson. Only the words that go in the blanks are given, since everyone will create different sentences.

My score for Exercise 5 is _____ out of 10.

VARIATIONS

The following words contain prefixes and suffixes. These prefixes and suffixes are used less often than the others you have studied so far, but they're still important—and they're easy to spell because they never change.

The following are words with the prefix *super*, meaning *above, over,* or *at the top of.*

superman   **super**ego   **super**human
superimpose **super**natural

The following are words with the prefix *sub*, meaning *under* or *below.*

subconscious **sub**contract **sub**sidiary

The following are words with the suffixes *er* and *ist.* These two endings indicate a person somehow associated with the root word.

perfection**ist**	therap**ist**	build**er**	design**er**
capital**ist**	radiolog**ist**	dwell**er**	biograph**er**
audiolog**ist**		vacation**er**	

There are many other prefixes and suffixes. Consult Appendix B for books that will help you continue improving your spelling.

Do you want more challenging words? Try these! Call on your study buddy to dictate them to you as you write them in your notebook.

Words in this challenge have the suffixes *ence* and *ance*. The challenge is that they both sound similar. In these two prefixes, the vowels take on the *schwa* sound.

ence	*ance*
audience	admittance
interdependence	hindrance
benevolence	allowance
convalescence	utterance
reference	appearance
	clearance

EXERCISE 6: WHAT HAVE YOU LEARNED?

Directions: Read each phrase **aloud.** Locate the base word that has a prefix and a suffix. Write only the base word on the line next to the phrase. It would be good practice to have your study buddy dictate these phrases to you.

1. disorderly conduct _____
2. citywide transportation _____
3. a biweekly payment _____
4. unreasonable behavior _____
5. thinking irrationally _____
6. interchangeable parts _____
7. unmanageable children _____
8. a disagreeable person _____
9. an interactive computer _____
10. an unprintable news account _____

Check your answers with the answer key at the end of this lesson.
My score for Exercise 6 is _____ out of 10.

ANSWER KEY FOR LESSON 17

Exercise 1

1. retraction
2. overpasses
3. presenting
4. unspeakable
5. interview
6. impure
7. distrustful
8. misstatement
9. instructive
10. impossible

Exercise 3

1. pass
2. place
3. polite
4. manage
5. view
6. pass
7. reason
8. trust
9. act
10. treat

Exercise 4

1. reaction
2. overpass
3. pretesting
4. unbreakable
5. interviewer

6. impolite
7. disgraceful
8. mistreatment
9. informative
10. impassable

Exercise 5

1. interviewer
2. reaction
3. mistreatment
4. impassable
5. pretesting
6. unbreakable
7. overpass
8. disgraceful
9. informative
10. impolite

Exercise 6

1. order
2. port
3. week (*payment* only has a suffix)
4. reason
5. rational
6. change
7. manage
8. agree
9. act
10. print

LESSON | 18

This lesson contains common and uncommon words that give spellers a hard time. We call them "spelling demons." What makes them so difficult is that they have no pattern. However, using the letter/sound relationship strategy will help you find those silent letters that just "hold a place."

SPELLING DEMONS

EXERCISE 1: EYEBALLING SPELLING LIST 18

Directions: Sweep your eyes across the line from left to right and back again. Do it quickly. Circle the word in each line that looks different from the others on that line.

Are you ready? Get set . . . Go!

1. doubt	doubt	drab	doubt
2. beauty	beauty	beauty	beautify
3. jeopardize	jeopardy	jeopardy	jeopardy
4. columns	clowns	columns	columns
5. answer	anther	answer	answer
6. freed	friend	friend	friend
7. diamond	domain	diamond	diamond

8. island	island	island	inland
9. scissors	scissors	sessions	scissors
10. acquire	acquaint	acquaint	acquaint

Check your answers with the answer key at the end of this lesson.
My score for Exercise 1 is _____ out of 10.

REFLECTION

Go back to the words that are the same on each line. Look at the words carefully. Which ones are a real spelling challenge for you?

_____

The words in this lesson don't have a sound pattern or common letters. That's why they are called "spelling demons." Move on to Sound Inventory to locate the silent letters that "just hold a place."

EXERCISE 2: SOUND INVENTORY

Directions: Read the words **aloud**. The words written using the letter/sound relationship will help you locate the silent letter or letters. Write the silent letter or letters on the provided space. The first one is done for you.

1. doubt	/d/ou/t/	_b_
2. beauty	/b/u/t/e/	_____
3. jeopardy	/j/e/p/ar/d/e/	_____
4. columns	/c/o/l/u/m/s/	_____
5. answer	/a/n/s/er/	_____
6. diamond	/d/i/m/o/n/d/	_____
7. island	/i/l/a/n/d/	_____
8. scissors	/s/i/z/or/z/	_____
9. acquaint	/a/k/w/a/n/t/	_____
10. friend	/f/r/e/n/d/	_____

Check your answers with the answer key at the end of the lesson.
My score for Exercise 2 is _____ out of 10.

EXERCISE 3: PRACTICE WITH SPELLING DEMONS

Directions: Read the words **aloud.** Then write the base word on the provided line.

1. doubtful   _____   **6.** islander   _____

2. answerable   _____   **7.** friendship   _____

3. columnist   _____   **8.** unanswerable   _____

4. friendly   _____   **9.** unfriendly   _____

5. friendless   _____   **10.** doubtfully   _____

Check your answers with the answer key at the end of this lesson.

My score for Exercise 3 is _____ out of 10.

EXERCISE 4: PRACTICE WRITING SPELLING LIST 18

Directions: Go back to Exercise 1. Look at the three words that are the same on each line. Write each of these words only once on the lines below. This would be a good time to have your study buddy dictate the words to you.

1. _____   **6.** _____

2. _____   **7.** _____

3. _____   **8.** _____

4. _____   **9.** _____

5. _____   **10.** _____

Consult your dictionary if the meaning of a word is unfamiliar to you.

Check your answers with the answer key at the end of this lesson.

My score for Exercise 4 is _____ out of 10.

EXERCISE 5: PRACTICE WRITING SPELLING LIST 18 IN CONTEXT

Directions: Use the words from Exercise 4 to complete the phrases below. For added practice, rewrite the entire phrase in your own sentence on the provided line.

1. _____ the question

_____

2. cutting paper with _____

_____

3. a tropical _____ resort

_____

4. a _____ engagement ring

_____

5. a trustworthy _____

_____

6. _____ on the front of a building

_____

7. The _____ of a sunset

_____

8. _____ yourself with a new friend

_____

9. _____ the word of a car salesman

_____

10. in danger or _____

_____

Check your answers with the answer key at the end of this lesson. Only the words that go in the blanks are given, since everyone will create different sentences.

My score for Exercise 5 is _____ out of 10.

VARIATIONS

In the following spelling demons, the base word changes when an ending is added. Notice how the final letters are usually dropped or changed when the suffix is added.

jeopardy	jeopardize		
beauty	beautify	beautiful	beautification
efficient	efficiency		
acquaint	acquaintance		
acquire	acquisition		

Do you want more challenging words? Read each of the following phrases aloud. Each underlined word is a spelling demon you should practice. These are more difficult than the first ten you learned. When you're sure you can spell these words, call on your study buddy to dictate the phrases to you.

succeeded in big <u>business</u>   <u>maneuver</u> the car into place
a fruit and <u>vegetable</u> market   a <u>psychic</u> reader
<u>lieutenant</u> in the Navy   <u>foreign</u> students

a <u>souvenir</u> from Holland   <u>sophomore</u> in high school
your driver's <u>license</u>   ill with <u>pneumonia</u>
a cash register <u>receipt</u>   <u>Wednesday</u> afternoon
a <u>convenience</u> store   daily <u>exercise</u>
the Teamster's <u>union</u>

EXERCISE 6: WHAT HAVE YOU LEARNED?

Directions: Complete each sentence with the correct form of the word.

1. The rain is so torrential that it's _____ whether the plane will arrive on time. (doubt, doubtful)
2. Your best _____ will comfort you. (friend, friendship)
3. The _____ necklace shimmered in the sunlight. (diamond, diamonds)
4. The soft light enhanced the model's _____. (beauty, beautiful)
5. Walking on railroad tracks will put your life in _____. (jeopardize, jeopardy)
6. The sharp _____ made a smooth cut. (scissor, scissors)
7. _____ of smoke billowed from the chimney. (columns, columnist)
8. Farming and tourism supported the people on the _____. (island, islanders)
9. You must _____ yourself with the information before you speak. (acquire, acquaint)
10. What is your _____ to the question? (answerable, answer)

Check your answers with the answer key at the end of this lesson.
My score for Exercise 6 is _____ out of 10.

ANSWER KEY FOR LESSON 18
Exercise 1

1. drab
2. beautify
3. jeopardize
4. clowns
5. anther
6. freed
7. domain
8. inland
9. sessions
10. acquire

Exercise 2

1. b
2. ea
3. o
4. n
5. w
6. a
7. s
8. c
9. c
10. i

Exercise 3

1. doubt
2. answer
3. column
4. friend
5. friend
6. island
7. friend
8. answer
9. friend
10. doubt

Exercise 4

1. doubt
2. beauty
3. jeopardy
4. columns
5. answer
6. friend
7. diamond
8. island
9. scissors
10. acquaint

Exercise 5

1. answer
2. scissors
3. island
4. diamond
5. friend
6. columns
7. beauty
8. acquaint
9. doubt
10. jeopardy

Exercise 6

1. doubtful
2. friend
3. diamond
4. beauty
5. jeopardy
6. scissors
7. columns
8. island
9. acquaint
10. answer

LESSON | 19

The English language is a flexible one. New words are being introduced continually to help us communicate about societal changes, technological advances, and so on. Sometimes the words themselves aren't new, but they take on a new meaning. This lesson introduces categories of words or phrases that reflect a **trend,** as well as words known as **mixed pairs.**

TRENDY WORDS AND MIXED PAIRS

EXERCISE 1: BECOMING FAMILIAR WITH TRENDY WORDS

Directions: Read each category of words. Pay careful attention to those that are underlined, and write them in the margin or make a list in your notebook. You'll be using them in a later exercise.

Words for Health
artificial sweetener
beta carotene
holistic medicine
fat free
cholesterol

Words for Technology
<u>cell</u> phone, cellular
on-line, computer
hard drive
key<u>board</u>, font
laser printer

Words for Health (cont.)

carbohydrates

protein

low impact aerobics

personal trainer, physical therapy

juicer, juice machine

vitamin therapy

pita bread

Words for Technology (cont.)

scanner

video, video camera

<u>byte</u>, megabyte

modem

satellite, satellite dish

cable elevision, <u>weather</u> channel

surfing the Internet

Words for Civil Service Employees

mail carrier (replaced mailman)

overnight express <u>mail</u>

priority mail

police officer (replaced policeman)

bias attack

child abuse

sexual harassment

firefighters (replaced firemen)

smoke inhalation

Words for Finance

junk bonds

automated teller machine (ATM)

home equity loan

individual retirement account (IRA)

<u>capital</u> gains

premium card

instant cash access

homeowner's insurance

Words for the Environment

pollution control

landfill <u>site</u>

sewage treatment

bottled water

compost, vermicomposting

<u>waste</u> management

Words for Politics and Society

in vitro fertilization

genetic engineering

paradigm shift

proactive/reactive

step family

sports utility vehicle

EXERCISE 2: UNDERSTANDING TRENDY WORDS

Directions: Use a word or phrase from the **Technology** category to best complete each sentence.

   1. There are over 100 _____ _____ channels.

   2. Hook up the _____ to the telephone line.

   3. A wireless phone is a _____ _____.

4. Copies from the _____ _____ are crisp and clear.

5. The greeting cards were printed in a Gothic _____.

Directions: Use a correct word or phrase from the **Health** category to best complete each sentence.

6. Sugar is being replaced by an _____ _____.

7. A round, pocket-like bread is known as _____.

8. After the surgery, you'll need _____ _____ to strengthen your leg muscles.

9. _____ _____ is a less conventional type of medical treatment.

10. Research suggests that large doses of _____ _____ will reduce the risk of some cancers.

Directions: Use a correct word or phrase from the **Civil Service** and **Finance** categories to best complete each sentence.

11. _____ _____ protects a family in the case of a fire or other disaster.

12. Even though the firefighters were protected, they still suffered from _____ _____.

13. You can withdraw cash from a bank any time of the day if you use the _____ _____ _____.

14. An _____ _____ _____ will guarantee money for your retirement.

15. Use _____ _____ _____ if you want that package delivered tomorrow.

Directions: Use a correct word or phrase from the **Politics and Society** and **Environment** categories to best complete each sentence.

16. _____ _____ can greatly alter the inheritance traits of future generations.

17. The Sanitation Department ships garbage to a _____ _____ almost daily.

18. Is _____ _____ safer to drink than tap water?

19. Autumn leaves become _____ for the spring planting.

20. To respond emotionally is reactive. To respond using a sequential thought process is _____.

Check your answers with the answer key at the end of this lesson. In your notebook, write the words from each list that you would like to learn. **My score for Exercise 2 is _____ out of 20.**

REFLECTION

What was your score for Exercise 2? _____

Did you have to look at the list on pages 163-164 to spell the answers correctly?_____

Write the words or phrases that you need to practice. _____

_____

You could probably spell most of the words correctly in Exercise 2. However, it is likely that you need practice on a few of them. In the next exercise, it's up to you to decide which words you'd like to study.

EXERCISE 3: SELECTING YOUR OWN SPELLING WORDS

Directions: From the results of Exercise 2 and the lists on page 163–164, select ten words you need to practice. Write them on the following lines.

1. _____   6. _____
2. _____   7. _____
3. _____   8. _____
4. _____   9. _____
5. _____   10. _____

Of course , if you need to study more than ten words, go ahead and do so. Don't be overwhelmed by a long list—take it one chunk at a time.

EXERCISE 4: PRACTICE WRITING SPELLING LIST 19 IN CONTEXT

Directions: Write a sentence for each word you chose in Exercise 3. Try to put more than one word in a sentence. For example: The *firefighters* were treated for *smoke inhalation.*

1. _____
2. _____
3. _____
4. _____
5. _____
6. _____

7. _____

8. _____

9. _____

10. _____

EXERCISE 5: READING THE MIXED PAIRS

Directions: Read the following pairs of words **aloud.** You'll discover that they sound the same. Do you know why they're spelled differently? Consult your dictionary for the answer to that question.

sell, cell	byte, bite	weather, whether	for, four
mail, male	whole, hole	capital, capitol	site, sight
board, bored	waste, waist		

These mixed pairs of words are often confused because they sound the same but have different meanings. There are many more of these in the English language. Most of these were chosen from the list on page 163-164. Reread each pair of words, and this time think of the letter/sound relationships as you read them. Are they consistent with the skills you learned in this book?

VARIATIONS

The following are more mixed pairs. How many of these are you familiar with already? Use your dictionary to see how spelling changes meaning.

base, bass	stationary, stationery	poor, pour, pore
hair, hare	peace, piece	right, write
seen, scene	break, brake	course, coarse
through, threw	principal, principle	there, their, they're

Do you want more challenging mixed pairs? Try these! Your study buddy can't dictate them to you this time. Since they sound the same, you wouldn't know which word to write! After you consult your dictionary just to be sure of the meanings, write each word in a sentence to cement the meaning in your mind.

assent, ascent	cannon, canon	cord, chord
council, counsel	compliment, complement	

EXERCISE 6: WHAT HAVE YOU LEARNED?

Directions: Complete each sentence with the correct word. Once you've filled in the blanks, have your study buddy dictate the completed sentences to you.

1. The _____ phone will _____ for $50.00. (sell, cell)

2. The newspaper was _____ for stating that the landfill _____ was a _____ for sore eyes. (sight, site, cited)

3. We were all tired and _____ at the community school _____ meeting. (board, bored)

4. The _____ report is uncertain. We don't know _____ to remain home or leave. (weather, whether)

5. Is the state _____ building the location of the vote on the _____ gains tax? (capital, capitol)

6. It's all right to _____ some of your dinner. If you eat too much, it will go right to your _____. (waist, waste)

7. The _____ delivery is expected at noon. (mail, male)

8. The courier will deliver the packages at _____ p.m. (for, four)

9. The computer's memory is measured in _____. (bites, bytes)

10. Who took a _____ out of my pita? (bite, byte)

Check your answers with the answer key at the end of this lesson.

My score for Exercise 6 is _____ out of 10.

ANSWER KEY FOR LESSON 19

Exercise 2

1. cable television
2. modem
3. cell phone
4. laser printer
5. font
6. artificial sweetener
7. pita
8. physical therapy
9. holistic medicine
10. beta carotene
11. homeowner's insurance
12. smoke inhalation
13. automated teller machine
14. individual retirement account
15. overnight express mail
16. genetic engineering
17. landfill site
18. bottled water
19. compost
20. proactive

Exercise 6

1. cell, sell
2. cited, site, sight
3. bored, board
4. weather, whether
5. capitol, capital
6. waste, waist
7. mail
8. four
9. bytes
10. bite

LESSON | 20

This lesson is a review of all the lessons you have covered in this book. You'll get the opportunity to practice spelling many of the words you have learned and see which ones you still need to work on.

PUTTING IT ALL TOGETHER

WHAT YOU'VE LEARNED

Congratulations! You've traveled a long way from Lesson 1. You should be a great speller by now. Review the lesson summaries below and see if there are any areas you feel you need to go back to.

- The lessons in this book provided you with a keen visual sense about the likenesses and differences of words. This was accomplished through the **EYEBALLING** exercises. For example, you saw there was a small visual difference between the words *conversation* and *conservation*.

- The lessons also provided you with a keen auditory sense about the sameness of sounds in words. This was accomplished through the **Sound Inventory** exercises. You heard the sameness in the words *oyster* and *oil*.

- Through practice with compound words, you picked up an important spelling skill. You learned that putting together two words spells one complex word. Bringing two words together is an easy skill to master and it expands your pool of spelling words. *Silverware* and *housekeeper* are examples of compound words.

- The lessons provided you with the letter/sound relationship strategy. You now know that letters represent sounds and sounds represent the language you want to write. Thus, the word *starve* can be heard as /s/t/ar/v/ and the word *remember* can be heard as /r/e/m/e/m/b/er/.

- You learned about hearing the rhythm of language by listening for the number of beats or syllables in a word. There are two syllables in the word *reject* and three in *rejection*.

- You also learned that stress can change the meaning and the form of a word. You know the difference between *des´ ert* and *de sert´*.

- The lessons provided you with the knowledge that the endings *s*, *es*, *ing*, and *ed* can tell the tense of a sentence, as in the words *jumps*, *brushes*, *waiting*, and *stayed*. The endings for the **amount** or **number of** are *s*, *es*, or *ies*, as in words like *keys*, *taxes*, and *stories*.

- You learned the important skill of focusing on the base word and building from it. **Prefixes** and **suffixes** are added to a base word to derive meaning. For instance, the base word *place* can be changed to *replace*, *replacement*, *displace*, and *replaceable*.

- You should now be aware of the importance of **context,** which can tell you the meaning and therefore the correct spelling of a word. Words such as *no* and *know*, and *made* and *maid* are known as **mixed pairs.** The words sound alike and follow the letter/sound relationship patterns, but it's the context that ultimately decides the correct form of the mixed pair.

- You also learned the sad fact that some words just do **not** follow a pattern or the letter/sound relationship. These "spelling demons" can only be conquered by practice and memorization.

There are two appendixes in this book that will help you even more. Appendix A is a complete list of spelling words in this book in alphabetical order, and a separate list of spelling demons. Appendix B lists books to use for further study.

Move on to the final exercises to check your spelling skills.

REVIEW EXERCISE 1

Directions: Read the words on each line from left to right. Circle the word that's misspelled in each line. Write the correct spelling in your notebook.

1. agents	aquaint	answer	bandstand
2. bangs	bartend	battere	billowing
3. beauty	beautifi	bouncers	boycott
4. bridge	bushes	bunches	selebrate
5. crums	cherish	cartoon	charmer
6. dewdrop	classes	conceev	conserve
7. cracker	county	country	dimond
8. disgraceful	dwells	decision	colums
9. deserting	composed	expresson	explore
10. fertile	frend	evolution	emotion

Check your answers with the answer key at the end of this lesson.

My score for Exercise 1 is _____ out of 10.

REVIEW EXERCISE 2

Directions: Read the words on each line from left to right. Circle the word that's misspelled in each line. Write the correct spelling in your notebook.

1. furnishes	gems	glory	graphefruit
2. glory	gnaws	homestile	inlet
3. impassable	interveiwer	lottery	impolite
4. labeling	lambes	limps	lodges
5. joepardy	keepsake	kneads	known
6. inspection	informative	lumber	misson
7. oisters	overpass	market	magic
8. palace	pashun	phantom	members
9. photograph	projected	pheesant	pawns
10. qualify	qarry	quit	raindrops

Check your answers with the answer key at the end of this lesson.

My score for Exercise 2 is _____ out of 10.

REVIEW EXERCISE 3

Directions: Read the words in each line from left to right. Circle the word that's misspelled in each line. Write the correct spelling in your notebook.

1. remote	rodeos	rythms	rhombus
2. robberes	rough	rowboat	reaction
3. shameful	sissors	slippers	slippery
4. sparklers	squirt	speres	starchy
5. sticker	stylish	shivver	shorten
6. swinging	stiff	stormy	stilish
7. unbreakible	thankful	upset	ushers
8. taxes	touched	terminates	sunlite
9. vertical	voyceless	whenever	wheel
10. waited	wrench	whisle	wrestling

Check your answers with the answer key at the end of this lesson.

~~My score for Exercise 3 is _____ out of 10.~~

You've come a long way since Lesson 1. You've done a great job of putting it all together. Although this is the end of the book, it's not the end of your spelling exercises. Becoming a better speller is a lifelong process. Here are a few suggestions for continuing to improve your skills:

- Keep your notebook active. Refer to it. Add to it.
- Pay attention to the written word no matter where you are. Eyeball advertisements on trains, buses, billboards, newspapers, store windows, menus, and supermarket flyers. Let no word escape you.
- There is one last message for you—*be word conscious!*

For further study, refer to the books listed in Appendix B.

ANSWER KEY FOR LESSON 20
Exercise 1

1. aquaint (acquaint)	**6.** conceev (conceive)
2. battere (battery)	**7.** dimond (diamond)
3. beautifi (beautify)	**8.** colums (columns)
4. selebrate (celebrate)	**9.** expresson (expression)
5. crums (crumbs)	**10.** frend (friend)

Exercise 2

1. graphefruit (grapefruit)
2. homestile (homestyle)
3. interveiwer (interviewer)
4. lambes (lambs)
5. joepardy (jeopardy)
6. misson (mission)
7. oisters (oysters)
8. pashun (passion)
9. pheesant (pheasant)
10. qarry (quarry)

Exercise 3

1. rythms (rhythms)
2. robberes (robberies)
3. sissors (scissors)
4. speres (spheres)
5. shivver (shiver)
6. stilish (stylish)
7. unbreakible (unbreakable)
8. sunlite (sunlight)
9. voyceless (voiceless)
10. whisle (whistle)

APPENDIX A

MASTER SPELLING LIST

This alphabetical list contains the words from Exercise 1 in Lessons 1–19. It also contains the words listed under **Variations** and **Challenge**. Use this list as a quick reference and as a study guide for practice and review.

account	admission	allowance	annoyance
accountable	admittance	almost	answer
acknowledgment	advisable	already	apathy
acquaint	aerobics	alteration	appearance
acquaintance	affirmation	although	applause
acquire	agents	altogether	aquatic
acquisition	airport	always	armory

article
ascent
assent
athletes
attainable
attorney
audience
audiologist
auditorium
August
authority
automated
automatic
automatically
average
awkward

badge
bandstand
bankrupt
bare
bartend
base
bass
batch
battery
bear
beautification
beautiful
beautify
beauty
bedpan
bedspread
believe
benevolence
benign
beta

billowing
biographer
birth
biscuit
bites
bluejay
board
boisterous
bold
book
bookkeeper
bored
bottled
boulder
bouncers
boycott
brake
bread
breadbasket
break
bridge
brilliant
brochure
brunch
budge
build
builder
bunches
business
byte

cable
calf
calves
campaign
candle
cannon

canon
capital
capitalist
capitol
care
cargo
carnivals
carotene
cartoon
cashing
catch
ceiling
celebrate
cell
cellophane
cell phone
cellular
cement
cemetery
centerpiece
chalk
chamois
channel
charmer
charter
chef
chemical
chemotherapy
chenille
cherish
cherries
cherry
chic
chief
chivalry
cholera
cholesterol

chord
chorus
Christian
Christmas
chromosome
cite
classification
classmate
clearance
cloister
coarse
cold
color
columns
commission
compartment
compatible
compile
complement
compliment
composed
composition
compost
compound
compression
compressor
computer
conceive
conclusion
concussion
confusion
conserve
constitution
convalescence
convenience
convertible
copied

copier	depletion	enjoyment	fasten
copies	depression	enough	feather
copy	deserting	equalization	featherbed
copying	design	equity	fertile
cord	designer	erode	fetch
council	desktop	eroded	fixate
counsel	dewdrop	erodes	floor
country	diamond	eroding	fold
county	discharge	erosion	for
couple	discussion	evolution	foreign
course	disgraceful	exact	fortitude
cracker	disguise	except	foundling
creditworthy	ditch	exceed	four
crook	doorway	exchange	friend
crowd	dormitory	exercise	fudge
crumbs	double	exhale	furnishes
curtain	doubt	exhaust	fusion
curve	dough	exhibit	
customer	dreads	existence	gangplank
cylinder	duo	exit	gargle
	duos	exonerate	gelatin
dare	Dutch	expandable	gems
daughter	dweller	expect	general
day	dwells	expensive	generate
days		experiment	generosity
dead	echo	exploit	genetic
deadbeat	echoes	explore	genocide
deaf	edge	export	Germany
debits	efficiency	expound	germicidal
December	efficient	expression	get
decent	eight	external	ghastly
decimate	either	extract	ghostly
decision	eligible	extraction	ghostwriter
deductible	emission		ghoulish
defamation	emotion	fair	gimmick
departure	employment	fallen	girl
deplete	engineering	familiar	glory

gnaws
gold
gore
grapefruit
graphic
graphing
graphite
grasshopper
group
grudge
guardianship
guess
guidance
guide
guitar
gymnasium
gyp
gypsy

hair
half
hallway
halter
halves
handset
happier
hard drive
hare
harpoon
harassment
hatch
head
health
hedge
heinous
heir
hemisphere

hey
high
hindrance
hitch
hold
holistic
homestyle
honeydew
honeysuckle
hood
hook
hotdog
hutch

igloo
igloos
illusion
impassable
implore
impolite
importation
impression
individual
inevitable
inexcusable
informative
inhalation
inlet
innocent
inspection
installation
institution
interdependence
internship
interviewer
invoice
island

jeopardize
jeopardy
judge

keepsake
key
keyboard
keys
kneads
knighthood
knowledge
knuckle

labeling
lambs
landfill
laptop
laser printer
latch
leaf
leaves
ledge
leisure
license
lieutenant
lilies
lily
limbs
listen
little
loaf
loaves
lodge
look
lore
lottery
lumber

machine
mail
male
mall
maneuver
market
match
matter
meant
medicine
members
memory
mess
mission
mistreatment
modem
moisten
moisture
mold
more
mortar
mourn
mummification
musical
mystery

nationalization
neighbor
neither
niece
nod
nodded
nods
normal
notification
notified
notifies

notify	pennies	population	recess
notifying	peculiar	pore	reference
	penny	potato	refrigerator
obey	percussion	potatoes	regardless
omission	perfectionist	poultry	rejoice
on-line	peripheral	pour	relief
oration	perishable	precision	relieve
orchestra	permission	pretesting	remarkable
organ	permit	principal	remote
organist	permits	principle	rendition
organization	permitted	printer	responsible
overnight	personal	proactive	restitution
overpass	personnel	process	retirement
oversight	phantom	profitable	revenge
overweight	pheasant	projected	rhetorical
overwhelm	phone	protein	rheumatism
oxide	phosphorus	provision	rhinestone
oxygen	photograph	psychic	rhinoceros
oysters	phrase	purple	rhombus
	physical		rhythms
pager	piece	qualify	ridge
paging	pita	quarry	right
palace	pitch	quicksand	riot
pamphlet	pleasant	quiet	robberies
paradigm	pledge	quintet	rodeo
participation	plunger	quit	rodeos
passbook	pneumonia	quite	rough
passion	poem		roughneck
passkey	poet	radio	router
password	pointers	radiologist	rowboat
patio	poise	radios	royalty
patios	poison	raindrops	ruin
pawns	police	reaction	
payable	pollution	ready	Sabbath
payday	pony	rebate	salesperson
peace	ponies	receipt	salt
peanut	poor	receive	satellite

sawdust	slippery	subcontract	thieves
scald	sludge	submit	thirsty
scanner	small	submitted	thirteenth
scene	smoke	submitting	thirty
scheduled	smooth	subsidiary	thorough
scissors	smudge	sunlight	though
scold	snitch	sunset	threw
score	snore	superego	through
scratch	sold	superhuman	tomato
seen	sophomore	superimpose	tomatoes
seize	soup	superman	took
sell	southbound	supernatural	torrential
sensible	souvenir	supervision	touched
sequels	sparkle	sweat	touchpad
sequence	sparklers	sweatband	tough
session	spell	sweatshop	toughen
sewage	spheres	swinging	tragedy
sexual	spicy	switch	transferable
shameful	spore	swore	transfusion
shelf	spread	sympathy	transmission
shelves	spreadsheet		transportation
ship	squirt	taxes	tray
shipped	stable	television	trays
shipping	stall	teller	trio
shiver	starchy	terminates	triumphant
shook	stationary	thankful	trouble
shoplifter	stationery	theatrical	turkey
shorten	steady	their	turkeys
shoulder	sticker	thematic	
sigh	stiff	therapist	unbreakable
sight	stitch	therapy	union
site	stood	there	uplift
sixteenth	store	thermometer	upset
sixty	stormy	thermostat	ushers
sketch	streamline	they	utterance
sleigh	stylish	they're	
slippers	subconscious	thief	vacation

vacationer	waste	white	worry
valiant	watch	whitewash	worse
variation	water	who	worship
varied	wealth	whole	worth
varies	wear	wholesale	worthwhile
vary	weather	wholesome	wrapper
vegetable	wedge	whom	wreath
vertical	Wednesday	whose	wrench
veto	weight	wicker	wrestling
vetoes	weightlifter	William	wrinkle
video	wheel	witch	wristband
vision	whenever	wood	write
vitamin	where	woodpecker	
voiceless	whether	wool	young
volleyball	whey	word	youth
	whimper	work	
waist	whimsical	workshop	zero
waited	whirlpool	world	zeroes
walnut	whisper	worldwide	
waltz	whistle	worm	

SPELLING DEMONS

The following words are frequently misspelled. Compile a list of words that are **your** spelling demons—words that seem to give you trouble all the time. Are these some of yours?

affect	environment	omitted
amateur	familiar	opinion
angel	February	playwright
angle	governor	prejudice
apparatus	heroine	professor
brilliant	judgment	recommend
clothes	library	religious
cylinder	nickel	separate
definite	occasional	vacuum
effect	occurrence	

APPENDIX B

RECOMMENDED BOOKS FOR FURTHER STUDY

Upon completion of this book, only you know what your additional needs are. You can visit your local public library or a book store for additional books on the topic of spelling. The books mentioned below are just a few suggestions.

- **If you need spelling rules to further understand why words are spelled a certain way,** then obtain a copy of this paperback with handy spelling rules.
  Spelling 101 by Claudia Sorsby (St. Martin's Press)
- **If you need a supplement to a dictionary,** then obtain a copy of *A Pocket Guide to Correct Spelling* by Francis Griffith (Barron's)

- **If you need a quick reference book to keep in your shirt pocket or pocketbook**, then obtain a copy of
  Webster's New World Mis-speller's Dictionary (Macmillan)
- **If you're ready to do more for your personal development in the areas of math, grammar, studying, writing, and reading**, look into the other books by LearningExpress. Order information is at the back of this book.